Everyman's Poetry

Everyman, I will go with thee,
and be thy guide

Matthew Arnold

Selected and edited by NICHOLAS SHRIMPTON

University of Oxford

EVERYMAN
J. M. Dent · London

This edition first published in Everyman Paperbacks in 1998
Selection, Introduction and other critical apparatus
© J. M. Dent 1998

J. M. Dent
Orion Publishing Group
Orion House
5 Upper St Martin's Lane
London
WC2H 9EA

Typeset by Deltatype Ltd, Birkenhead, Merseyside
Printed in Great Britain by
The Guernsey Press Co. Ltd., Guernsey, C. I.

British Library Cataloguing-in-Publication
Data is available on request

ISBN 0 46087 961 8

Contents

From **Merope. A Tragedy** (1858)

From **New Poems** (1867)

From **Poems** (1877)

Note on the Author and Editor

MATTHEW ARNOLD was born at Laleham in 1822. His father, Dr Thomas Arnold, was a teacher and clergyman who subsequently became famous as the reforming headmaster of Rugby School. Educated at Rugby and at Balliol College, Oxford, Arnold became a Fellow of Oriel College in 1845. This was a non-teaching post which he combined from April 1847 with a job as private secretary to the Marquis of Lansdowne, a cabinet minister in the Whig government of Lord John Russell. He published his first volume of poems, *The Strayed Reveller*, anonymously in 1849. In 1851 he married Frances Lucy Wightman and took a full-time job as an Inspector of Schools; he became Chief Inspector in 1884, finally retiring in 1886. In 1852 he published his second volume of verse, *Empedocles on Etna and Other Poems*, but came almost immediately to disapprove of the title poem. In 1853 he replaced it with a new volume of *Poems* containing a long preface to explain the suppression of 'Empedocles on Etna' and a poem which demonstrated his new, more classical ideal of English poetry: 'Sohrab and Rustum'. In 1857 he became Professor of Poetry at Oxford, a part-time post which he occupied with distinction for ten years. In the 1860s he began to publish his Oxford lectures on literature, following them by the end of the decade with a number of important works of social and cultural criticism, of which *Culture and Anarchy* is the best known. In the 1870s he published three controversial books on theological topics, seeking to redefine Christianity for a sceptical modern age. The first collected edition of his poems appeared in 1869. Though he wrote few new poems after that date, he continued to revise his earlier work and his popular *Selected Poems* was reprinted almost annually from 1878 onwards. Arnold died in Liverpool in 1888.

NICHOLAS SHRIMPTON is Fellow and Tutor in English at Lady Margaret Hall, Oxford. He is the co-editor of *The Whole Music of Passion: New Essays on Swinburne* and has written widely on nineteenth-century literature, especially Ruskin, Swinburne, the Rossettis and Arnold.

Chronology of Arnold's Life

Year	Age	Life
1822		(24 December) Birth of Matthew Arnold, eldest son of Thomas Arnold and Mary Penrose, at Laleham, Middlesex
1828	5	Thomas Arnold appointed headmaster of Rugby
1834	11	Fox How built as family holiday home in the Lake District. Wordsworth a friendly neighbour
1836	13	Pupil at Winchester
1837	14	Pupil at Rugby School
1840	17	School prize poem *Alaric at Rome* published. Wins scholarship to Balliol College, Oxford
1841	18	Thomas Arnold becomes Oxford Professor of Modern History. Matthew goes up to Balliol in October; friendship with A. H. Clough
1842	19	Death of Thomas Arnold (12 June)
1843	20	Newdigate Prize poem *Cromwell* published
1844	21	Writes 'Shakspeare' sonnet (August). Second Class Honours in Oxford Finals (November)
1845	22	Elected Fellow of Oriel College (March). Philosophical reading includes Lucretius, Cudworth, Glanvil and the *Bhagavad-Gita*
1846	23	Trips to France to see George Sand and Rachel
1847	24	Reading Béranger, Maurice de Guérin. To London as secretary to Lord Lansdowne (Whig cabinet minister) (April). Possible *tendresse* for Lake District neighbour Mary Claude

Chronology of his Times

Year	Artistic Events	Historical Events
1822	Death of Shelley	Greek War of Independence
1828	Carlyle, *Essay on Goethe*	Repeal of Test Acts
1834	Death of Coleridge	New Poor Law
1836	Dickens, *Pickwick Papers*	Hampden controversy
1837	Carlyle, *French Revolution*	Accession of Queen Victoria
1840	Browning, *Sordello*	Victoria marries Albert
1841	Browning, *Pippa Passes*	Newman, *Tract 90*. Tory government (Peel)
1842	Tennyson, *Poems*	Chartist petition
1843	Mill, *Logic* Carlyle, *Past & Present*	Newman resigns St Mary's
1844	E. B. Barrett, *Poems*	Stanley, *Life of Arnold*
1845	Browning, *Dramatic Romances & Lyrics*	Newman joins Roman Church. Irish famine (1845–50)
1846	Brontës, Poems Dickens, *Dombey and Son*	Repeal of Corn Laws. Whig government (Russell)
1847	Brontës, *Wuthering Heights, Jane Eyre* Tennyson, *The Princess*	Irish emigration. Swiss Civil War

Year	Age	Life
1848	25	Reading Epictetus. Visits Switzerland (September); writes first of love poems later included in the 'Switzerland' sequence. Reads Senancour's *Obermann* (November)
1849	26	Publishes *The Strayed Reveller, and Other Poems* (February). At work on 'Empedocles on Etna' (July); publishes 'To the Hungarian Nation' in the *Examiner*. Holiday in Switzerland (September); writes 'Stanzas in Memory of the Author of "Obermann" '
1850	27	Wordsworth dies (April); Arnold's elegy 'Memorial Verses' in *Fraser's* (August). Arnold's sister Jane marries; his courtship of Frances Lucy Wightman discouraged by her father
1851	28	Engaged to Miss Wightman (March). Appointed Inspector of Schools (April). Marriage. (June) Honeymoon on Continent; visits Grande Chartreuse (September) Begins work as inspector of Non-Conformist schools (11 October)
1852	29	First child, Thomas, born (July) Publishes *Empedocles on Etna, and Other Poems* (October)
1853	30	Clough compares the *Empedocles* volume unfavourably with Alexander Smith's *A Life-Drama* because it lacks engagement with modern life (July). Arnold publishes *Poems A New Edition*; preface explains he has suppressed 'Empedocles on Etna', not because it lacked modernity, but because it failed to 'inspirit and rejoice the reader'. 'Sohrab and Rustum' replaces the previous title-poem (November)
1854	31	Publishes revised edition of *Poems* (1853). *Poems, Second Series* (December) (dated 1855)

Year	Artistic Events	Historical Events
1848	Pre-Raphaelite Brotherhood Clough, *Bothie of Toperna-Fuosich* Keats, *Life & Letters*	Revolutions in France, Germany, Poland, Hungary, Italy. Young Ireland rising. Chartist meeting in London
1849	Dickens, *David Copperfield* Sainte-Beuve, *Causeries du lundi*	European revolutions suppressed. British annex Punjab
1850	Tennyson, *In Memoriam* Wordsworth, *The Prelude*	Roman Catholic bishops re-established in England
1851	E. B. Browning, *Casa Guidi Windows*	Whig government resigns but returns. Great Exhibition
1852	Thackeray, *Henry Esmond* Gautier, *Émaux et Camées* Leconte de Lisle, *Poèmes antiques*	Tory government (Derby) Whig & Peelite government (Aberdeen)
1853	C. Brontë, *Villette* Alexander Smith, *Poems*	Russia attacks Turkey
1854	Aytoun, *Firmilian* Patmore, *The Angel in the House*	Crimean War (1854–6)

Year	Age	Life
1855	32	Publishes 'Stanzas from the Grande Chartreuse' (April), 'Haworth Churchyard' (May) in *Fraser's*
1856	33	Member of the Athenaeum. Finds himself 'sadly bothered and hindered' from writing poetry
1857	34	Publishes a third, further revised edition of *Poems* (1853). Inaugural lecture as Oxford Professor of Poetry (November); series on 'The Modern Element in Literature' (on medieval and Romantic writing) runs until spring 1863. *Merope. A Tragedy* (December) (dated 1858)
1858	35	Settles in Chester Square, London. Holiday in France and Switzerland; visits Heine's grave
1859	36	To Continent for Newcastle Education Commission; meets Renan and Sainte-Beuve. *England and the Italian Question* (August)
1860	37	'Saint Brandan' in *Fraser's* and 'The Lord's Messengers' in *Cornhill* (July). Oxford lectures on translating Homer
1861	38	*On Translating Homer* (January) *The Popular Education of France* (May). Clough dies; Arnold gives further Homer lecture (November)
1862	39	Publishes 'The Twice-Revised Code' (*Fraser's*, March) and *On Translating Homer: Last Words*
1863	40	Lecture on Heine to begin third Oxford series (June). Lecture on Joubert (November)

Year	Artistic Events	Historical Events
1855	Browning, *Men & Women* Tennyson, *Maud*	Palmerston government
1856	Morris & Rossetti, *Oxford & Cambridge Magazine* E. B. Browning, *Aurora Leigh*	Anglo-Persian War
1857	Hughes, *Tom Brown's Schooldays* Baudelaire, *Les Fleurs du mal*	Indian Mutiny. Commercial crisis
1858	Clough, *Amours de Voyage* Morris, *The Defence of Guenevere*	Tory government (Derby)
1859	Tennyson, *Idylls of the King* Fitzgerald, *Rubáiyát* George Eliot, *Adam Bede*	War of Italian Liberation. Liberal government (Palmerston). Darwin, *Origin of Species*. Mill, *On Liberty*
1860	Dickens, *Great Expectations*	Garibaldi in Sicily. *Essays & Reviews*
1861	George Eliot, *Silas Marner* Hughes, *Tom Brown at Oxford* Morris & Co	American Civil War (1861–5). Prince Consort dies. First Italian parliament meets
1862	C. Rossetti, *Goblin Market* Swinburne's review of Baudelaire Meredith, *Modern Love* Clough, *Poems*	Bismarck becomes chief minister of Prussia. Revised education code ('payment by results')
1863	Gilchrist, *Life of Blake*	Renan, *Vie de Jésus*. Bishop Colenso deposed

Year	Age	Life
1864	41	*A French Eton*. Oxford lecture 'The Function of Criticism' (October)
1865	42	Publishes *Essays in Criticism* (February). Visits Continent for Taunton Commission schools enquiry (April–November). Begins fourth Oxford lecture series on 'The Study of Celtic Literature' (December)
1866	43	'My Countrymen' in *Cornhill* (February). 'Thyrsis' in *Macmillan's* (April). Publishes first of the *Friendship's Garland* essays (July)
1867	44	*On the Study of Celtic Literature* (June); final Oxford lecture: 'Culture & Its Enemies'. *New Poems* (July)
1868	45	Deaths of sons Basil and Thomas. Second, revised edition of *New Poems* (May) Publishes *Culture and Anarchy* essays in *Cornhill*
1869	46	*Culture and Anarchy* (January). *Poems*, the first collected edition of his poetry (June)
1870	47	Promoted Senior Inspector of Schools. *St Paul and Protestantism* (May)
1871	48	*Friendship's Garland* (February)
1873	50	*Literature & Dogma* (February)
1875	52	*God & the Bible* (November)
1877	54	*Last Essays on Church & Religion* (March)

Year	Artistic Events	Historical Events
1864	Browning, *Dramatis Personae* Newman, *Apologia pro vita sua* Tennyson, *Enoch Arden*	Prussia and Austria annex Schleswig-Holstein
1865	Swinburne, *Atalanta in Calydon*	Palmerston dies; Russell PM
1866	Swinburne, *Poems & Ballads* C. Rossetti, *The Prince's Progress*	Prussia defeats Austria. Gladstone's Reform Bill defeated. Tory government (Derby). Hyde Park riots
1867	Morris, *Life & Death of Jason* Pater, *Essay on Winckelmann*	Second Reform Act. Fenian rising. Marx, *Das Kapital*
1868	Browning, *The Ring & the Book* Swinburne, *William Blake* Morris, *The Earthly Paradise*	Disraeli succeeds Derby as PM. Liberal government (Gladstone). Russia annexes Samarcand
1869	Tennyson, *The Holy Grail & Other Poems*	Suez Canal opens. Mill, *The Subjection of Women*
1870	D. G. Rossetti, *Poems* Newman, *The Grammar of Assent*	Franco-Prussian War. Forster's Elementary Education Act
1871	Swinburne, *Songs before Sunrise* George Eliot, *Middlemarch*	Commune in Paris. Abolition of religious tests at Oxford and Cambridge
1873	Pater, *The Renaissance*	German troops leave France
1874	Hardy, *Far from the Madding Crowd*	Tory government (Disraeli). T. H. Green, *Hume*
1877	Mallock, *The New Republic*	Queen Victoria proclaimed Empress of India

Year	Age	Life
1878	55	*Selected Poems* (June) Begins three-year series of articles on Ireland (July)
1879	56	*Mixed Essays* and a selected *Wordsworth*
1880	57	Contributes 'The Study of Poetry' and essays on Gray and Keats to Ward's *English Poets*
1881	58	Publishes a selected *Byron*
1882	59	'Westminster Abbey' in *The Nineteenth Century* (January) *Irish Essays* (March)
1884	61	Promoted Chief Inspector of Schools
1885	62	*Discourses in America*; final collected *Poems*
1886	63	Retires from Inspectorship
1888	65	Dies in Liverpool (15 April) *Essays in Criticism (2nd Series)* published (November)

Year	Artistic Events	Historical Events
1878	Swinburne, *Poems & Ballads, 2nd Series*	Treaty of Berlin
1880	Death of George Eliot	Liberal government (Gladstone)
1881	James, *Portrait of a Lady* Wilde, *Poems*	Irish Coercion and Land Acts
1882	Swinburne, *Tristram of Lyonesse*	Lord Frederick Cavendish murdered in Phoenix Park
1885	Pater, *Marius the Epicurean*	Third Reform Act. Tory government (Salisbury)
1886	Hardy, *The Mayor of Casterbridge* Kipling, *Departmental Ditties*	Liberal government (Gladstone). Irish Home Rule Bill defeated. Tory government (Salisbury)
1888	Mrs Humphry Ward, *Robert Elsmere* Morris, *Signs of Change* Yeats, *Fairy Tales of the Irish Peasantry*	Accession of Kaiser Wilhelm II

Introduction

Matthew Arnold said in 1869 that his poems represented 'the main movement of mind of the last quarter of a century'[1]. The claim points directly to the intellectual and referential qualities of Arnold's verse. He was a poet of statement, committed to the proposition that poetry should have things of specific and substantial interest to say about the world.

Born in 1822, Arnold grew up at a time when English poetry was being reinvented after the early deaths of Keats, Shelley and Byron. Arthur Hallam, in 1831, divided contemporary poets into a Wordsworthian school of 'reflective' writers and a new group, led by Alfred Tennyson, of 'poets of sensation'.[2] Arnold remained unashamedly a poet of reflection. He believed that 'modern poetry can only subsist by its *contents*' and that it was chiefly of value when it was 'an adequate respresentation and interpretation' of its era. Poetry should both mimetically reflect, and intellectually reflect upon, the world of events and ideas. Literature was 'a criticism of life'.[3]

Late Victorian symbolists, like their predecessors among the poets of sensation, would reject this. For them poetry was not a criticism of life but 'a revelation of a hidden life'.[4] But reflective poetry has its own distinctive virtues. As Henry James would remark in 1865, 'the merit which pre-eminently characterises Mr Arnold's poems' is the merit of 'having a *subject*'.[5]

Arnold never wavered in his commitment to the poetry of statement. But he was by no means unaware of the handicaps that it imposed. Writing a poetry of ideas meant that he was always likely to have, in his own words, 'less poetical sentiment than Tennyson'. His further commitment to expressing only those ideas that he could whole-heartedly endorse limited his range, leaving him with 'less intellectual vigour and abundance than Browning'.[6] It also obliged him to revise, or even suppress, some of his most interesting work. 'The Neckan', first published in 1853, had its meaning entirely reversed in 1869. 'Empedocles on Etna' was rejected by Arnold within a year of its first appearance and was only reprinted (significantly, at Browning's suggestion) after an absence of fourteen years.

As this suggests, Arnold's poetry can sometimes be stiff, dry and discordant. The reflective poet, in Hallam's words, 'will be apt to mistake the pleasure he has in knowing a thing to be true, for the pleasure he would have in knowing it to be beautiful'. This tendency is made worse by the fact that Arnold's ear is imperfect. Despite the formal interests demonstrated by his pioneering experiments with free verse, his sense of verbal sound can be uncertain, his diction and imagery worryingly imprecise.

But imperfection is not the same thing as failure. Arnold's auditory imagination operates intermittently, sometimes failing but sometimes working with marvellous sureness. He can produce effects as awkward as the tongue-twister that opens the sonnet 'To a Friend': 'Who prop, thou ask'st, in these bad days, my mind?'. He can also write verse lines as perfectly judged as 'The unplumb'd, salt, estranging sea' (in 'To Marguerite. Continued'), where 'salt' interrupts, with ideal congruity, both the rhythm and the referential register. Varying the line with a trochaic substitution, 'salt' breaks into the intellectual discourse of 'unplumb'd' (the world is beyond the scope of our understanding) and 'estranging' (no human being can ever fully know another) with a sharply physical specification of the saline quality of the sea and, by implication, human tears. Writing like this helps to explain why a poet so seemingly remote from Matthew Arnold as Sylvia Plath could have received her first inspiration from his work. Listening, as a child, to her mother's reading of 'The Forsaken Merman', Plath says, 'A spark flew off Arnold and shook me like a chill. I wanted to cry; I felt very odd. I had fallen into a new way of being happy.'[7]

'The Forsaken Merman' reminds us also that the Arnoldian poetry of ideas did not require a direct mode of statement. He could and did produce poems as baldly reflective as 'To a Friend', and his willingness to use dramatic personae declined in the 1850s. But his imagination continued to work most freely when enacting ideas in narrative. 'The Forsaken Merman' borrows a Danish folk-tale to articulate the pain caused, within families or between lovers, by the clash of faith and unbelief. 'Dover Beach' will use autobiographical and historical story (Arnold's marriage and the Peloponnesian War) to fix its distinctive moment of the 'movement of mind'.

As that phrase suggests, Arnold's topic was a process of change, a movement not a state of mind. This is why this relatively explicit poetry can sometimes be hard to understand. Arnold believed different things at different times. Occasionally a change of view would be so strong that he would feel obliged to suppress or radically revise a poem. More frequently he would allow successive poems, in his own words, 'to represent . . . the main movement' of ideas in his era. Arnold's first volume of poems, *The Strayed Reveller*, published in 1849, is a striking example of this. The title poem, like 'Mycerinus' and 'The Forsaken Merman', expresses an Epicurean philosophy which insists upon the claims of pleasure. Reacting against the religious controversies that dominated English intellectual life in the mid-1840s, Arnold constructs an irreligious and hedonic alternative. The Reveller rejects the model of the suffering Romantic artist in favour of a poetics of pleasure and intoxication. Mycerinus, disillusioned by the injustice of the gods, turns to a life of incessant physical enjoyment. The Merman and his children, abandoned by their Christian mother, return to the pagan depths of the sea.

But these poems were written before the spring of 1848 when Arnold, as the secretary of a cabinet minister, found himself obliged to confront human suffering of exceptional severity. In Ireland the government of which he was, however humbly, a servant was struggling to cope with the horrors of the famine. Abroad (and potentially at home), ministers were witnessing a year of violent revolutions. Arnold's first volume of verse, despite its title, ends by expressing a Stoic philosophy. The answer to the question 'Who prop, thou ask'st, in these bad days, my mind' is, of course, in large part Epictetus. The closing poem 'Resignation. To Fausta' articulates a view of the world that acknowledges the significance of suffering. This is not a return to religion: the universe is animated, in this modern understanding, by a sinister 'something that infects the world'. But asserting the claims of pleasure is no longer enough. The 'general lot' is no 'milder' because we forget the truths suggested by contemporary science and political experience. The adequate response is 'to bear rather than rejoice'.

A Stoic volume with an Epicurean title poem is not an easy thing to make sense of, and Arnold's own family was puzzled by it. Writing to his sister Jane, in March 1849, Arnold confessed that 'The true reason why parts suit you while others do not is that my poems are fragments i.e. that I am fragments.'[8] His next collection,

Empedocles on Etna, and Other Poems, in 1852, was, however, once again a record of different phases of belief. Arnold's 1848 Stoicism proved hard to sustain. In 1849, under the pressure of political and personal distress, it gave way to a gloomier philosophy. Arnold turned to Senancour, Foscolo and Byron for his ideas and literary models. Poems like 'Too Late' and 'Despondency' are characteristic of this period. Though 'Empedocles on Etna' includes the 'Chant' in which its hero articulates a resolutely Stoic theory, the poem's suicidal conclusion is the most extreme expression of the Byronic mood, and Arnold soon came to disapprove of it.

'Stanzas in Memory of the Author of "Obermann" ', written in November 1849, was actually a farewell to Senancour's world-weariness. Thereafter, Arnold would turn, not just back to Stoicism, but towards an increasingly positive version of the Stoic creed. In November 1853 *Empedocles on Etna, and Other Poems* was replaced by a volume simply entitled *Poems. A New Edition.* Arnold prefaced this 1853 collection with a Neo-Aristotelian manifesto for modern poetry. Poetry should be mimetic: 'a representation which is . . . particular, precise, and firm'.[9] Literature derived its importance from its choice of topic, and the best topic was a narrative of events: 'actions; human actions; possessing an inherent interest in themselves'. Such actions did not need modern settings, and the design, or architectonics, of the poem took precedence over the felicity of individual lines. Since poetry's purpose was pleasure, however, situations that were 'morbid' were unsuitable even for tragedy. Ancient Greek poetry provided the appropriate model. The subjective focus and suicidal outcome of 'Empedocles on Etna' gave way to the new procedures of 'Sohrab and 'Rustum'.

Arnold's new poetics do not, as has sometimes been suggested, constitute a retreat from poetic difficulty. 'Sohrab and Rustum' remains profoundly painful: a father unwittingly kills his long-lost son. But the topic is treated in the manner of classical epic rather than the Romantic egotistical sublime, and human suffering is presented as something that must be positively accepted. Some of the poems in the 1852 collection had already been based on this combination of classical formal models and fortifying views, most notably the songs sung by Callicles in 'Empedocles on Etna'. One of these, 'Cadmus and Harmonia', survived in the 1853 volume. The other four were put back into print two years later as 'The Harp Player on Etna.'

These lyrics attempt, like the 'O Son and Mother' chorus of Arnold's 1858 verse play *Merope*, to address painful experience in a spirit of serene acceptance. 'Cadmus and Harmonia', for example, alludes to tragic events while stressing the consoling power of art and the possibility of a real, though unillusioned, peace of mind. The bleak modern understanding of the human condition is fully acknowledged: Arnold even retains in his 1855 volume one key section of Empedocles's scientific statement, as 'The Philosopher and the Stars'. The Byronic rebelliousness of Typho and Marsyas, however, is rebuked. Art, the servant of Apollo, hymns not disturbance but 'the Father/Of all things . . . The Stars in their calm'.

Despite the success of these neo-classical (and currently rather under-valued) poems, the 1853 Preface was not Arnold's last word on poetics, and his poetry continued to change. In 1857, in his lecture on 'The Modern Element in Literature', he expressed his conception of the need for poetry to be 'adequate'. With the publication of 'The Scholar Gipsy' in 1853, he had already begun to give new elegance, and a new depth of narrative interest, to the direct engagement with contemporary issues previously seen in poems like 'Resignation'. Three further examples were first collected in his *New Poems* of 1867: 'Stanzas from the Grande Chartreuse', 'Thyrsis', and 'Dover Beach'.

These poems make allusive use of Greek pastoral or Romantic nature poetry. But all are firmly set in the mid-nineteenth century and their distinction lies in their ability to express a deeply felt yet curiously unsubjective sense of the modern condition. 'The Scholar Gipsy', for example, revisits the hunger for Romantic withdrawal but does so in terms that place the possibility of an alternative to contemporary experience irretrievably in the past. 'Dover Beach', like the 'Switzerland' sequence which Arnold only finally completed in 1877, uses fragments of autobiography to problematise a general condition. The possibility of human affection is simultaneously asserted and erased, in a love poetry that remains hauntingly conscious that, in a modern understanding, 'We mortal millions live *alone*' and the universal context of love is now a 'darkling plain'. Arnold remains committed to the poetry of statement. But he writes it, at his best, at an exceptionally high level of subtlety and seriousness.

NICHOLAS SHRIMPTON

References

1 Letter to his mother, 12 June 1869, printed in G. W. Russell, *Letters of Matthew Arnold 1848–1888*, 2 vols, Macmillan 1895, 2.9.

2 Hallam's essay, originally in the *Englishman's Magazine*, August 1831, is reprinted in J. D. Jump, *Tennyson, The Critical Heritage*, Routledge and Kegan Paul 1967, 34–49.

3 See Arnold's letter to A. H. Clough, 28 October 1852, printed in C. Y. Lang, *The Letters of Matthew Arnold*, Vol. 1, University Press of Virginia 1996, 245; 'On the Modern Element in Literature', R. W. Super, ed. *The Complete Prose Works of Matthew Arnold*, 11 vols, University of Michigan Press 1960–77, 1.29; 'Joubert', Super, 3.209.

4 W. B. Yeats, quoted in F. O. Matthiessen, *The Achievement of T. S. Eliot*, 1935, reprinted OUP 1969, 90.

5 James's article, originally in the *North American Review*, July 1865, is reprinted in C. Dawson & J. Pfordresher, *Matthew Arnold, Prose Writings, The Critical Heritage*, Routledge and Kegan Paul, 1979, 142–50.

6 Letter to his mother, 12 June 1869.

7 A. S. Plath, *Letters Home by Sylvia Plath*, Harper and Row 1975, 31–2, quoting 'Ocean 1212-W' in S. Plath, *Johnny Panic and the Bible of Dreams*, Faber 1977, 21.

8 Letter to Jane Martha Arnold, 17 March 1849, printed Lang, 1.143.

9 For the full text of Arnold's 1853 Preface see Super, 1. 1–15.

Note on the Text

The texts are those of the first appearances of the poems in book form. The poems are arranged according to the volumes in which they first thus appeared, and for the most part in the order in which they appeared in those volumes. The exceptions are the poems in *The Strayed Reveller* (1849), where the original order gives a particularly confusing sense of Arnold's intellectual development. 'Cadmus and Harmonia', 'The Harp Player on Etna', and 'The Philosopher and the Stars' had previously appeared in book form as part of *Empedocles on Etna*; they are here given in the text of their first independent appearance. Some of the poems in the 'Switzerland' sequence had appeared in book form as early as 1852, and a sequence with this title first appeared in 1853; the sequence is here given in the text of *Poems* (1877), the point at which Arnold finally determined the form and plot of the poem.

Matthew Arnold

from **The Strayed Reveller, and Other Poems** (1849)

The Strayed Reveller

A YOUTH. CIRCE

THE YOUTH

Faster, faster,
O Circe, Goddess,
Let the wild, thronging train,
The bright procession
Of eddying forms,
Sweep through my soul.

Thou standest, smiling
Down on me; thy right arm
Lean'd up against the column there,
Props thy soft cheek;   10
Thy left holds, hanging loosely,
The deep cup, ivy-cinctur'd,
I held but now.

Is it then evening
So soon? I see, the night dews,
Cluster'd in thick beads, dim
The agate brooch-stones
On thy white shoulder.
The cool night-wind, too,
Blows through the portico,   20
Stirs thy hair, Goddess,
Waves thy white robe.

CIRCE

Whence art thou, sleeper?

THE YOUTH

When the white dawn first
Through the rough fir-planks
Of my hut, by the chestnuts,
Up at the valley-head,
Came breaking, Goddess,
I sprang up, I threw round me
    My dappled fawn-skin: 30
Passing out, from the wet turf,
Where they lay, by the hut door,
I snatch'd up my vine-crown, my fir-staff
    All drench'd in dew:
    Came swift down to join
    The rout early gather'd
    In the town, round the temple,
        Iacchus' white fane
        On yonder hill.

Quick I pass'd, following   40
The wood-cutters' cart-track
Down the dark valley; – I saw
On my left, through the beeches,
    Thy palace, Goddess,
    Smokeless, empty:
Trembling, I enter'd; beheld
    The court all silent,
    The lions sleeping;
    On the altar, this bowl.
    I drank, Goddess –   50
And sunk down here, sleeping,
On the steps of thy portico.

CIRCE

Foolish boy! Why tremblest thou?
Thou lovest it, then, my wine?
Wouldst more of it? See, how glows,

Through the delicate flush'd marble,
  The red creaming liquor,
  Strown with dark seeds!
Drink, then! I chide thee not,
  Deny thee not my bowl.   60
Come, stretch forth thy hand, then – so, –
  Drink, drink again!

THE YOUTH

Thanks, gracious One!
Ah, the sweet fumes again!
  More soft, ah me!
  More subtle-winding
  Than Pan's flute-music.
  Faint – faint! Ah me!
Again the sweet sleep.

CIRCE

Hist! Thou – within there!   70
  Come forth, Ulysses!
Art tired with hunting?
While we range the woodland,
  See what the day brings.

ULYSSES

Ever new magic!
Hast thou then lur'd hither,
  Wonderful Goddess, by thy art,
  The young, languid-ey'd Ampelus,
  Iacchus' darling –
Or some youth belov'd of Pan,   80
  Of Pan and the Nymphs?
That he sits, bending downward
His white, delicate neck
To the ivy-wreath'd marge
Of thy cup:–the bright, glancing vine-leaves
  That crown his hair,
Falling forwards, mingling
With the dark ivy-plants;

His fawn-skin, half untied,
Smear'd with red wine-stains? Who is he,   90
   That he sits, overweigh'd
   By fumes of wine and sleep,
   So late, in thy portico?
What youth, Goddess, – what guest
   Of Gods or mortals?

CIRCE

Hist! he wakes!
I lur'd him not hither, Ulysses.
   Nay, ask him!

THE YOUTH

Who speaks? Ah! Who comes forth
To thy side, Goddess, from within?   100
   How shall I name him?
This spare, dark-featur'd,
   Quick-ey'd stranger?
Ah! and I see too
His sailor's bonnet,
His short coat, travel-tarnish'd,
   With one arm bare. –
Art thou not he, whom fame
   This long time rumours
The favour'd guest of Circe, brought by the waves?   110
   Art thou he, stranger?
   The wise Ulysses,
   Laertes' son?

ULYSSES

I am Ulysses.
And thou, too, sleeper?
   Thy voice is sweet.
It may be thou hast follow'd
Through the islands some divine bard,
   By age taught many things,
   Age and the Muses;   120
   And heard him delighting

The chiefs and people
In the banquet, and learn'd his songs,
    Of Gods and Heroes,
    Of war and arts,
    And peopled cities
    Inland, or built
By the grey sea. – If so, then hail!
    I honour and welcome thee.

THE YOUTH

The Gods are happy.   130
They turn on all sides
Their shining eyes:
And see, below them,
The Earth, and men.

They see Tiresias
Sitting, staff in hand,
    On the warm, grassy
    Asopus' bank:
His robe drawn over
His old, sightless head: 140
    Revolving inly
    The doom of Thebes.

They see the Centaurs
In the upper glens
Of Pelion, in the streams,
    Where red-berried ashes fringe
    The clear-brown shallow pools;
    With streaming flanks, and heads
    Rear'd proudly, snuffing
    The mountain wind.   150

They see the Indian
Drifting, knife in hand,
His frail boat moor'd to
A floating isle thick matted
With large-leav'd, low-creeping melon-plants,
And the dark cucumber.

He reaps, and stows them,
Drifting – drifting: – round him,
Round his green harvest-plot,
Flow the cool lake-waves: 160
The mountains ring them.

They see the Scythian
On the wide Stepp, unharnessing
His wheel'd house at noon.
He tethers his beast down, and makes his meal,
Mares' milk, and bread
Bak'd on the embers:– all around
The boundless waving grass-plains stretch, thick-starr'd
With saffron and the yellow hollyhock
And flag-leav'd iris flowers.   170
Sitting in his cart
He makes his meal: before him, for long miles,
Alive with bright green lizards,
And the springing bustard fowl,
The track, a straight black line,
Furrows the rich soil: here and there
Clusters of lonely mounds
Topp'd with rough-hewn
Grey, rain-blear'd statues, overpeer
The sunny Waste.   180

They see the Ferry
On the broad, clay-laden
Lone Chorasmian stream: thereon
With snort and strain,
Two horses, strongly swimming, tow
The ferry-boat, with woven ropes
To either bow
Firm-harness'd by the mane: – a chief,
With shout and shaken spear
Stands at the prow, and guides them: but astern,   190
The cowering Merchants, in long robes,
Sit pale beside their wealth
Of silk-bales and of balsam-drops,
Of gold and ivory,

Of turquoise-earth and amethyst,
    Jasper and chalcedony,
And milk-barr'd onyx stones.
The loaded boat swings groaning
    In the yellow eddies.
        The Gods behold them.   200

They see the Heroes
Sitting in the dark ship
On the foamless, long-heaving,
    Violet sea:
At sunset nearing
The Happy Islands.
These things, Ulysses,
The wise Bards also
Behold and sing.
But oh, what labour!   210
    O Prince, what pain!

They too can see
Tiresias: – but the Gods,
Who give them vision,
Added this law:
That they should bear too
    His groping blindness,
    His dark foreboding,
    His scorn'd white hairs.
Bear Hera's anger   220
Through a life lengthen'd
To seven ages.

They see the Centaurs
On Pelion: – then they feel,
They too, the maddening wine
Swell their large veins to bursting: in wild pain
    They feel the biting spears
Of the grim Lapithæ, and Theseus, drive,
Drive crashing through their bones: they feel
High on a jutting rock in the red stream   230
    Alcmena's dreadful son

Ply his bow: — such a price
　　The Gods exact for song;
To become what we sing.

　　They see the Indian
　On his mountain lake: — but squalls
Make their skiff reel, and worms
I' the unkind spring have gnaw'd
Their melon-harvest to the heart: They see
　　The Scythian: — but long frosts　　　　　　240
Parch them in winter-time on the bare Stepp,
Till they too fade like grass: they crawl
　　Like shadows forth in spring.

　　They see the Merchants
　On the Oxus' stream: — but care
Must visit first them too, and make them pale.
　　Whether, through whirling sand,
A cloud of desert robber-horse has burst
Upon their caravan: or greedy kings,
In the wall'd cities the way passes through,　　250
　　Crush'd them with tolls: or fever-airs,
　　　On some great river's marge,
　　　Mown them down, far from home.

　　They see the Heroes
　Near harbour: — but they share
Their lives, and former violent toil, in Thebes,
　　Seven-gated Thebes, or Troy:
　　　Or where the echoing oars
　　　Of Argo, first,
Startled the unknown Sea.　　　　　　　　　260

　　The old Silenus
　Came, lolling in the sunshine,
　From the dewy forest coverts,
　　This way, at noon.
Sitting by me, while his Fauns
　　Down at the water side
　　Sprinkled and smooth'd

His drooping garland,
He told me these things.

But I, Ulysses,   270
Sitting on the warm steps,
Looking over the valley,
All day long, have seen,
Without pain, without labour,
Sometimes a wild-hair'd Mænad;
Sometime a Faun with torches;
And sometimes, for a moment,
Passing through the dark stems
Flowing-rob'd – the belov'd,
The desir'd, the divine,   280
Belov'd Iacchus.

Ah cool night-wind, tremulous stars!
Ah glimmering water –
Fitful earth-murmur –
Dreaming woods!
Ah golden-hair'd strangely-smiling Goddess,
And thou, prov'd, much enduring,
Wave-toss'd Wanderer!
Who can stand still?
Ye fade, ye swim, ye waver before me.   290
The cup again!

Faster, faster,
O Circe, Goddess,
Let the wild thronging train,
The bright procession
Of eddying forms,
Sweeps through my soul!

Mycerinus

'Not by the justice that my father spurn'd,
Not for the thousands whom my father slew,
Altars unfed and temples overturn'd,
Cold hearts and thankless tongues, where thanks were due;
Fell this late voice from lips that cannot lie,
Stern sentence of the Powers of Destiny.

I will unfold my sentence and my crime.
My crime, that, rapt in reverential awe,
I sate obedient, in the fiery prime
Of youth, self-govern'd, at the feet of Law;   10
Ennobling this dull pomp, the life of kings,
By contemplation of diviner things.

My father lov'd injustice, and liv'd long;
Crown'd with grey hairs he died, and full of sway.
I lov'd the good he scorn'd, and hated wrong:
The Gods declare my recompense to-day.
I look'd for life more lasting, rule more high;
And when six years are measur'd, lo, I die!

Yet surely, o my people, did I deem
Man's justice from the all-just Gods was given: 20
A light that from some upper fount did beam,
Some better archetype, whose seat was heaven;
A light that, shining from the blest abodes,
Did shadow somewhat of the life of Gods.

Mere phantoms of man's self-tormenting heart,
Which on the sweets that woo it dares not feed:
Vain dreams, that quench our pleasures, then depart,
When the dup'd soul, self-master'd, claims its meed:
When, on the strenuous just man, Heaven bestows,
Crown of his struggling life, an unjust close.   30

Seems it so light a thing then, austere Powers,
To spurn man's common lure, life's pleasant things?

Seems there no joy in dances crown'd with flowers,
Love, free to range, and regal banquettings?
Bend ye on these, indeed, an unmov'd eye,
Not Gods but ghosts, in frozen apathy?

Or is it that some Power, too wise, too strong,
Even for yourselves to conquer or beguile,
Whirls earth, and heaven, and men, and gods along,
Like the broad rushing of the column'd Nile?   40
And the great powers we serve, themselves may be
Slaves of a tyrannous Necessity?

Or in mid-heaven, perhaps, your golden ears,
Where earthly voice climbs never, wing their flight,
And in wild hunt, through mazy tracts of stars,
Sweep in the sounding stillness of the night?
Or in deaf ease, on thrones of dazzling sheen,
Drinking deep draughts of joy, ye dwell serene?

Oh wherefore cheat our youth, if thus it be,
Of one short joy, one lust, one pleasant dream?   50
Stringing vain words of powers we cannot see,
Blind divinations of a will supreme;
Lost labour: when the circumambient gloom
But hides, if Gods, Gods careless of our doom?

The rest I give to joy. Even while I speak
My sand runs short; and as yon star-shot ray,
Hemm'd by two banks of cloud, peers pale and weak,
Now, as the barrier closes, dies away;
Even so do past and future intertwine,
Blotting this six years' space, which yet is mine.   60

Six years – six little years – six drops of time –
Yet suns shall rise, and many moons shall wane,
And old men die, and young men pass their prime,
And languid Pleasure fade and flower again;
And the dull Gods behold, ere there are flown,
Revels more deep, joy keener than their own.

Into the silence of the groves and woods
I will go forth; but something would I say –
Something – yet what I know not: for the Gods
The doom they pass revoke not, nor delay;   70
And prayers, and gifts, and tears, are fruitless all,
And the night waxes, and the shadows fall.

Ye men of Egypt, ye have heard your king.
I go, and I return not. But the will
Of the great Gods is plain; and ye must bring
Ill deeds, ill passions, zealous to fulfil
Their pleasure, to their feet; and reap their praise,
The praise of Gods, rich boon! and length of days.'

– So spake, he, half in anger, half in scorn;
And one loud cry of grief and of amaze   80
Broke from his sorrowing people: so he spake;
And turning, left them there; and with brief pause,
Girt with a throng of revellers, bent his way
To the cool region of the groves he lov'd.
There by the river banks he wander'd on,
From palm-grove on to palm-grove, happy trees,
Their smooth tops shining sunwards, and beneath
Burying their unsunn'd stems in grass and flowers:
Where in one dream the feverish time of Youth
Might fade in slumber, and the feet of Joy   90
Might wander all day long and never tire:
Here came the king, holding high feast, at morn
Rose-crown'd; and ever, when the sun went down,
A hundred lamps beam'd in the tranquil gloom,
From tree to tree, all through the twinkling grove,
Revealing all the tumult of the feast,
Flush'd guests, and golden goblets, foam'd with wine;
While the deep-burnish'd foliage overhead
Splinter'd the silver arrows of the moon.
   It may be that sometimes his wondering soul   100
From the loud joyful laughter of his lips
Might shrink half startled, like a guilty man
Who wrestles with his dream; as some pale Shape,

Gliding half hidden through the dusky stems,
Would thrust a hand before the lifted bowl,
Whispering, 'A little space, and thou art mine.'
It may be on that joyless feast his eye
Dwelt with mere outward seeming; he, within,
Took measure of his soul, and knew its strength,
And by that silent knowledge, day by day,   110
Was calm'd, ennobled, comforted, sustain'd.
It may be; but not less his brow was smooth,
And his clear laugh fled ringing through the gloom,
And his mirth quail'd not at the mild reproof
Sigh'd out by Winter's sad tranquility;
Nor, pall'd with its own fulness, ebb'd and died
In the rich languor of long summer days;
Nor wither'd, when the palm-tree plumes that roof'd
With their mild dark his grassy banquet-hall,
Bent to the cold winds of the showerless Spring;   120
No, nor grew dark when Autumn brought the clouds.
   So six long years he revell'd, night and day;
And when the mirth wax'd loudest, with dull sound
Sometimes from the grove's centre echoes came,
To tell his wondering people of their king;
In the still night, across the steaming flats,
Mix'd with the murmur of the moving Nile.

The Forsaken Merman

Come, dear children, let us away;
   Down and away below.
Now my brothers call from the bay;
Now the great winds shorewards blow;
Now the salt tides seawards flow;
Now the wild white horses play,
Champ and chafe and toss in the spray.
   Children dear, let us away.
     This way, this way.

Call her once before you go.   10
    Call once yet.
In a voice that she will know:
    'Margaret! Margaret!'
Children's voices should be dear
(Call once more) to a mother's ear:
Children's voices, wild with pain.
    Surely she will come again.
Call her once and come away.
    This way, this way.
'Mother dear, we cannot stay.'   20
The wild white horses foam and fret.
    Margaret! Margaret!

Come, dear children, come away down.
    Call no more.
One last look at the white-wall'd town,
And the little grey church on the windy shore.
    Then come down.
She will not come though you call all day.
    Come away, come away.

Children dear, was it yesterday   30
We heard the sweet bells over the bay?
    In the caverns where we lay,
   Through the surf and through the swell
The far-off sound of a silver bell?
Sand-strewn caverns, cool and deep,
Where the winds are all asleep;
Where the spent lights quiver and gleam;
Where the salt weed sways in the stream;
Where the sea-beasts rang'd all round
Feed in the ooze of their pasture-ground;   40
Where the sea-snakes coil and twine,
Dry their mail and bask in the brine;
Where great whales come sailing by,
Sail and sail, with unshut eye,
Round the world for ever and aye?

When did music come this way?
Children dear, was it yesterday?

Children dear, was it yesterday
(Call yet once) that she went away?
Once she sate with you and me,   50
On a red gold throne in the heart of the sea,
And the youngest sate on her knee.
She comb'd it's bright hair, and she tended it well,
When down swung the sound of the far-off bell.
She sigh'd, she look'd up through the clear green sea.
She said; 'I must go, for my kinsfolk pray
In the little grey church on the shore to-day.
'Twill be Easter-time in the world – ah me!
And I lose my poor soul, Merman, here with thee.'
I said; 'Go up, dear heart, through the waves.   60
Say thy prayer, and come back to the kind sea-caves.'
    She smil'd, she went up through the surf in the bay.
        Children dear, was it yesterday?

    Children dear, were we long alone?
'The sea grows stormy, the little ones moan.
Long prayers,' I said, 'in the world they say.
Come,' I said, and we rose through the surf in the bay.
We went up the beach, by the sandy down
Where the sea-stocks bloom, to the white-wall'd town.
Through the narrow pav'd streets, where all was still,   70
To the little grey church on the windy hill.
From the church came a murmur of folk at their prayers,
But we stood without in the cold blowing airs.
We climb'd on the graves, on the stones, worn with rains,
And we gaz'd up the aisle through the small leaded panes.
    She sate by the pillar; we saw her clear:
    'Margaret, hist! come quick, we are here.
    Dear heart,' I said, 'we are long alone.
    The sea grows stormy, the little ones moan.'
But, ah, she gave me never a look,   80
For her eyes were seal'd to the holy book.
    'Loud prays the priest; shut stands the door.'

Come away, children, call no more.
Come away, come down, call no more.

  Down, down, down.
  Down to the depths of the sea.
She sits at her wheel in the humming town,
  Singing most joyfully.
Hark, what she sings; 'O joy, o joy,
For the humming street, and the child with its toy. 90
For the priest, and the bell, and the holy well.
  For the wheel where I spun,
  And the blessed light of the sun.'
 And so she sings her fill,
 Singing most joyfully,
 Till the shuttle falls from her hand,
 And the whizzing wheel stands still.
She steals to the window, and looks at the sand;
 And over the sand at the sea;
 And her eyes are set in a stare; 100
 And anon there breaks a sigh,
 And anon there drops a tear,
 From a sorrow-clouded eye,
 And a heart sorrow-laden,
  A long, long sigh.
For the cold strange eyes of a little Mermaiden.
 And the gleam of her golden hair.

Come away, away children.
Come children, come down.
The salt tide rolls seaward. 110
Lights shine in the town.
She will start from her slumber
When gusts shake the door;
She will hear the winds howling,
Will hear the waves roar.
We shall see, while above us
The waves roar and whirl,
A ceiling of amber,
A pavement of pearl.

Singing, 'Here came a mortal,   120
But faithless was she.
And alone dwell for ever
The kings of the sea.'

But, children, at midnight,
When soft the winds blow;
When clear falls the moonlight;
When spring-tides are low:
When sweet airs come seaward
From heaths starr'd with broom;
And high rocks throw mildly   130
On the blanch'd sands a gloom:
Up the still, glistening beaches,
Up the creeks we will hie;
Over banks of bright seaweed
The ebb-tide leaves dry.
We will gaze, from the sand-hills,
At the white, sleeping town;
At the church on the hill-side –
    And then come back down.
Singing, 'There dwells a lov'd one,   140
But cruel is she.
She left lonely for ever
The kings of the sea.'

To a Friend

Who prop, thou ask'st, in these bad days, my mind?
He much, the old man, who clearest-soul'd of men,
Saw The Wide Prospect, and the Asian Fen,
And Tmolus' hill, and Smyrna's bay, though blind.
Much he, whose friendship I not long since won,
That halting slave, who in Nicopolis
Taught Arrian, when Vespasian's brutal son

Clear'd Rome of what most sham'd him. But be his
My special thanks, whose even-balanc'd soul,
From first youth tested up to extreme old age,   10
Business could not make dull, nor Passion wild:
Who saw life steadily, and saw it whole:
The mellow glory of the Attic stage;
Singer of sweet Colonus, and its child.

Resignation

To Fausta

'To die be given us, or attain!
Fierce work it were, to do again.'
So pilgrims, bound for Mecca, pray'd
At burning noon: so warriors said,
Scarf'd with the cross, who watch'd the miles
Of dust that wreath'd their struggling files
Down Lydian mountains: so, when snows
Round Alpine summits eddying rose,
The Goth, bound Rome-wards: so the Hun,
Crouch'd on his saddle, when the sun   10
Went lurid down o'er flooded plains
Through which the groaning Danube strains
To the drear Euxine: so pray all,
Whom labours, self-ordain'd, enthrall;
Because they to themselves propose
On this side the all-common close
A goal which, gain'd, may give repose.
So pray they: and to stand again
Where they stood once, to them were pain;
Pain to thread back and to renew   20
Past straits, and currents long steer'd through.

   But milder natures, and more free;
Whom an unblam'd serenity

Hath freed from passions, and the state
Of struggle these necessitate;
Whom schooling of the stubborn mind
Hath made, or birth hath found, resign'd;
These mourn not, that their goings pay
Obedience to the passing day.
These claim not every laughing Hour 30
For handmaid to their striding power;
Each in her turn, with torch uprear'd,
To await their march; and when appear'd,
Through the cold gloom, with measur'd race,
To usher for a destin'd space,
(Her own sweet errands all foregone)
The too imperious Traveller on.
These, Fausta, ask not this: nor thou,
Time's chafing prisoner, ask it now.

We left, just ten years since, you say, 40
That wayside inn we left to-day:
Our jovial host, as forth we fare,
Shouts greeting from his easy chair;
High on a bank our leader stands,
Reviews and ranks his motley bands;
Makes clear our goal to every eye,
The valley's western boundary.
A gate swings to: our tide hath flow'd
Already from the silent road.
The valley pastures, one by one, 50
Are threaded, quiet in the sun:
And now beyond the rude stone bridge
Slopes gracious up the western ridge.
Its woody border, and the last
Of its dark upland farms is past:
Lone farms, with open-lying stores,
Under their burnish'd sycamores.
All past: and through the trees we glide
Emerging on the green hill-side.
There climbing hangs, a far-seen sign, 60
Our wavering, many-colour'd line;
There winds, upstreaming slowly still

Over the summit of the hill.
And now, in front, behold outspread
Those upper regions we must tread;
Mild hollows, and clear heathy swells,
The cheerful silence of the fells.
Some two hours' march, with serious air,
Through the deep noontide heats we fare:
The red-grouse, springing at our sound,   70
Skims, now and then, the shining ground;
No life, save his and ours, intrudes
Upon these breathless solitudes.
O joy! again the farms appear;
Cool shade is there, and rustic cheer:
There springs the brook will guide us down,
Bright comrade, to the noisy town.
Lingering, we follow down: we gain
The town, the highway, and the plain.
And many a mile of dusty way,   80
Parch'd and road-worn, we made that day;
But, Fausta, I remember well
That, as the balmy darkness fell,
We bath'd our hands, with speechless glee,
That night, in the wide-glimmering Sea.

Once more we tread this self-same road,
Fausta, which ten years since we trod:
Alone we tread it, you and I;
Ghosts of that boisterous company.
Here, where the brook shines, near its head,   90
In its clear, shallow, turf-fring'd bed;
Here, whence the eye first sees, far down,
Capp'd with faint smoke, the noisy town;
Here sit we, and again unroll,
Though slowly, the familiar whole.
The solemn wastes of heathy hill
Sleep in the July sunshine still:
The self-same shadows now, as then,
Play through this grassy upland glen:
The loose dark stones on the green way   100
Lie strewn, it seems, where then they lay:

On this mild bank above the stream,
(You crush them) the blue gentians gleam.
Still this wild brook, the rushes cool,
The sailing foam, the shining pool. –
These are not chang'd: and we, you say,
Are scarce more chang'd, in truth, than they.

The Gipsies, whom we met below,
They too have long roam'd to and fro.
They ramble, leaving, where they pass,   110
Their fragments on the cumber'd grass.
And often to some kindly place
Chance guides the migratory race
Where, though long wanderings intervene,
They recognise a former scene.
The dingy tents are pitch'd: the fires
Give to the wind their wavering spires;
In dark knots crouch round the wild flame
Their children, as when first they came;
They see their shackled beasts again   120
Move, browsing, up the grey-wall'd lane.
Signs are not wanting, which might raise
The ghosts in them of former days:
Signs are not wanting, if they would;
Suggestions to disquietude.
For them, for all, Time's busy touch,
While it mends little, troubles much:
Their joints grow stiffer; but the year
Runs his old round of dubious cheer:
Chilly they grow; yet winds in March,   130
Still, sharp as ever, freeze and parch:
They must live still; and yet, God knows,
Crowded and keen the country grows:
It seems as if, in their decay,
The Law grew stronger every day.
So might they reason; so compare,
Fausta, times past with times that are.
But no: – they rubb'd through yesterday
In their hereditary way;
And they will rub through, if they can,   140

To-morrow on the self-same plan;
Till death arrives to supersede,
For them, vicissitude and need.

   The Poet, to whose mighty heart
Heaven doth a quicker pulse impart,
Subdues that energy to scan
Not his own course, but that of Man.
Though he move mountains; though his day
Be pass'd on the proud heights of sway;
Though he hath loos'd a thousand chains;   150
Though he hath borne immortal pains;
Action and suffering though he know;
– He hath not liv'd, if he lives so.
He sees, in some great-historied land,
A ruler of the people stand;
Sees his strong thought in fiery flood
Roll through the heaving multitude;
Exults: yet for no moment's space
Envies the all-regarded place.
Beautiful eyes meet his; and he   160
Bears to admire uncravingly:
They pass; he, mingled with the crowd,
Is in their far-off triumphs proud.
From some high station he looks down,
At sunset, on a populous town;
Surveys each happy group that fleets,
Toil ended, through the shining streets;
Each with some errand of its own;–
And does not say, 'I am alone.'
He sees the gentle stir of birth   170
When Morning purifies the earth;
He leans upon a gate, and sees
The pastures, and the quiet trees.
Low woody hill, with gracious bound,
Folds the still valley almost round;
The cuckoo, loud on some high lawn,
Is answer'd from the depth of dawn;
In the hedge straggling to the stream,
Pale, dew-drench'd, half-shut roses gleam:

But where the further side slopes down 180
He sees the drowsy new-wak'd clown
In his white quaint-embroider'd frock
Make, whistling, towards his mist-wreath'd flock;
Slowly, behind the heavy tread,
The wet flower'd grass heaves up its head. –
Lean'd on his gate, he gazes: tears
Are in his eyes, and in his ears
The murmur of a thousand years:
Before him he sees Life unroll,
A placid and continuous whole; 190
That general Life, which does not cease,
Whose secret is not joy, but peace;
That Life, whose dumb wish is not miss'd
If birth proceeds, if things subsist:
The Life of plants, and stones, and rain:
The Life he craves; if not in vain
Fate gave, what Chance shall not controul,
His sad lucidity of soul.

You listen: – but that wandering smile,
Fausta, betrays you cold the while. 200
Your eyes pursue the bells of foam
Wash'd, eddying, from this bank, their home.
'Those Gipsies,' so your thoughts I scan,
'Are less, the Poet more, than man.
They feel not, though they move and see:
Deeply the Poet feels; but he
Breathes, when he will, immortal air,
Where Orpheus and where Homer are.
In the day's life, whose iron round
Hems us all in, he is not bound. 210
He escapes thence, but we abide.
Not deep the Poet sees, but wide.'
The World in which we live and move
Outlasts aversion, outlasts love.
Outlasts each effort, interest, hope,
Remorse, grief, joy: – and were the scope
Of these affections wider made,
Man still would see, and see dismay'd,

Beyond his passion's widest range
Far regions of eternal change.   220
Nay, and since death, which wipes out man,
Finds him with many an unsolv'd plan,
With much unknown, and much untried,
Wonder not dead, and thirst not dried,
Still gazing on the ever full
Eternal mundane spectacle;
This World in which we draw out breath,
In some sense, Fausta, outlasts death.

    Blame thou not therefore him, who dares
Judge vain beforehand human cares.   230
Whose natural insight can discern
What through experience others learn.
Who needs not love and power, to know
Love transient, power an unreal show.
Who treads at ease life's uncheer'd ways:—
Him blame not, Fausta, rather praise.
Rather thyself for some aim pray
Nobler than this – to fill the day.
Rather, that heart, which burns in thee,
Ask, not to amuse, but to set free.   240
Be passionate hopes not ill resign'd
For quiet, and a fearless mind.
And though Fate grudge to thee and me
The Poet's rapt security,
Yet they, believe me, who await
No gifts from Chance, have conquer'd Fate.
They, winning room to see and hear,
And to men's business not too near,
Through clouds of invidual strife
Draw homewards to the general Life.   250
Like leaves by suns not yet uncurl'd:
To the wise, foolish; to the world,
Weak: ye not weak, I might reply,
Not foolish, Fausta, in His eye,
Each moment as it flies, to whom,
Crowd as we will its neutral room,
Is but a quiet watershed

Whence, equally, the Seas of Life and Death are fed.

    Enough, we live:– and if a life,
With large results so little rife,   260
Though bearable, seem hardly worth
This pomp of worlds, this pain of birth;
Yet, Fausta, the mute turf we tread,
The solemn hills around us spread,
This stream that falls incessantly,
The strange-scrawl'd rocks, the lonely sky,
If I might lend their life a voice,
Seem to bear rather than rejoice.
And even could the intemperate prayer
Man iterates, while these forbear,   270
For movement, for an ampler sphere.
Pierce Fate's impenetrable ear;
Not milder is the general lot
Because our spirits have forgot,
In action's dizzying eddy whirl'd,
The something that infects the world.

from **Empedocles on Etna, and Other Poems** (1852)

Too Late

Each on his own strict line we move,
And some find death ere they find love:
So far apart their lives are thrown
From the twin soul that halves their own.

And sometimes, by still harder fate,
The lovers meet, but meet too late.
– Thy heart is mine! – True, true! ah true! –
Then, love, thy hand! – Ah no! adieu!

Destiny

Why each is striving, from of old,
To love more deeply than he can?
Still would be true, yet still grows cold?
– Ask of the Powers that sport with man!

They yok'd in him, for endless strife,
A heart of ice, a soul of fire;
And hurl'd him on the Field of Life,
An aimless unallay'd Desire.

Despondency

The thoughts that rain their steady glow
Like stars on life's cold sea,
Which others know, or say they know –
They never shone for me.

Thoughts light, like gleams, my spirit's sky,
But they will not remain;
They light me once, they hurry by,
And never come again.

Stanzas

In memory of the author of 'Obermann'

In front the awful Alpine track
Crawls up its rocky stair;
The autumn storm-winds drive the rack
Close o'er it, in the air.

Behind are the abandoned baths
Mute in their meadows lone;
The leaves are on the valley paths;
The mists are on the Rhone –

The white mists rolling like a sea.
I hear the torrents roar.
– Yes, Obermann, all speaks of thee!   10
I feel thee near once more.

I turn thy leaves: I feel their breath
Once more upon me roll;
That air of languor, cold, and death,
Which brooded o'er thy soul.

Fly hence, poor Wretch, whoe'er thou art,
Condemn'd to cast about,
All shipwreck in thy own weak heart,
For comfort from without: 20

A fever in these pages burns
Beneath the calm they feign;
A wounded human spirit turns
Here, on its bed of pain.

Yes, though the virgin mountain air
Fresh through these pages blows,
Though to these leaves the glaciers spare
The soul of their mute snows,

Though here a mountain murmur swells
Of many a dark-bough'd pine,   30
Though, as you read, you hear the bells
Of the high-pasturing kine –

Yet, through the hum of torrent lone,
And brooding mountain bee,
There sobs I know not what ground tone
Of human agony.

Is it for this, because the sound
Is fraught too deep with pain,
That, Obermann! the world around
So little loves thy strain?   40

Some secrets may the poet tell,
For the world loves new ways.
To tell too deep ones is not well;
It knows not what he says.

Yet of the spirits who have reign'd
In this our troubled day,
I know but two, who have attain'd,
Save thee, to see their way.

By England's lakes, in grey old age,
His quiet home one keeps;   50
And one, the strong much-toiling Sage,
In German Weimar sleeps.

But Wordsworth's eyes avert their ken
From half of human fate;
And Goethe's course few sons of men
May think to emulate.

For he pursued a lonely road,
His eyes on nature's plan;
Neither made man too much a God,
Nor God too much a man.   60

Strong was he, with a spirit free
From mists, and sane, and clear;
Clearer, how much! than ours: yet we
Have a worse course to steer.

For though his manhood bore the blast
Of a tremendous time,
Yet in a tranquil world was pass'd
His tenderer youthful prime.

But we, brought forth and rear'd in hours
Of change, alarm, surprise –   70
What shelter to grow ripe is ours?
What leisure to grow wise?

Like children bathing on the shore,
Buried a wave beneath,
The second wave succeeds, before
We have had time to breathe.

Too fast we live, too much are tried,
Too harass'd, to attain
Wordsworth's sweet calm, or Goethe's wide
And luminous view to gain.   80

And then we turn, thou sadder sage!
To thee: we feel thy spell.
The hopeless tangle of our age –
Thou too hast scann'd it well.

Immoveable thou sittest; still
As death; compos'd to bear.
Thy head is clear, thy feeling chill –
And icy thy despair.

Yes, as the Son of Thetis said,
One hears thee saying now –　　　　　　　　　　　　　　90
'Greater by far than thou are dead:
Strive not: die also thou.' –

Ah! Two desires toss about
The poet's feverish blood.
One drives him to the world without.
And one to solitude.

The glow of thought, the thrill of life –
Where, where do these abound?
Not in the world, not in the strife
Of men, shall they be found.　　　　　　　　　　　　　　100

He who hath watch'd, not shar'd, the strife,
Knows how the day hath gone;
He only lives with the world's life
Who hath renounc'd his own.

To thee we come, then. Clouds are roll'd
Where thou, O Seer, art set;
Thy realm of thought is drear and cold –
The world is colder yet!

And thou hast pleasures too to share
With those who come to thee:　　　　　　　　　　　　　　110
Balms floating on thy mountain air,
And healing sights to see.

How often, where the slopes are green
On Jaman, hast thou sate
By some high chalet door, and seen
The summer day grow late,

And darkness steal o'er the wet grass
With the pale crocus starr'd,
And reach that glimmering sheet of glass
Beneath the piny sward,   120

Lake Leman's waters, far below:
And watch'd the rosy light
Fade from the distant peaks of snow:
And on the air of night

Heard accents of the eternal tongue
Through the pine branches play:
Listen'd, and felt thyself grow young;
Listen'd, and wept – Away!

Away the dreams that but deceive!
And thou, sad Guide, adieu!   130
I go; Fate drives me: but I leave
Half of my life with you.

We, in some unknown Power's employ,
Move on a rigorous line:
Can neither, when we will, enjoy;
Nor, when we will, resign.

I in the world must live: – but thou,
Thou melancholy Shade!
Wilt not, if thou can'st see me now,
Condemn me, nor upbraid.   140

For thou art gone away from earth,
And place with those dost claim,
The Children of the Second Birth
Whom the world could not tame;

And with that small transfigur'd Band,
Whom many a different way
Conducted to their common land,
Thou learn'st to think as they.

Christian and pagan, king and slave,
Soldier and anchorite,   150
Distinctions we esteem so grave,
Are nothing in their sight.

They do not ask, who pin'd unseen,
Who was on action hurl'd,
Whose one bond is, that all have been
Unspotted by the world.

There without anger thou wilt see
Him who obeys thy spell
No more, so he but rest, like thee,
Unsoil'd: – and so, Farewell!   160

Farewell! – Whether thou now liest near
That much-lov'd inland sea,
The ripples of whose blue waves cheer
Vevey and Meillerie,

And in that gracious region bland,
Where with clear-rustling wave
The scented pines of Switzerland
Stand dark round thy green grave,

Between the dusty vineyard walls
Issuing on that green place,   170
The early peasant still recalls
The pensive stranger's face,

And stoops to clear thy moss-green date
Ere he plods on again:
Or whether, by maligner fate,
Among the swarms of men.

Where between granite terraces
The Seine conducts her wave,
The Capital of Pleasure sees
Thy hardly heard of grave –   180

Farewell! Under the sky we part,
In this stern Alpine dell.
O unstrung will! O broken heart!
A last, a last farewell!

from **Poems** (1853)

Sohrab and Rustum

An episode

And the first grey of morning fill'd the east,
And the fog rose out of the Oxus stream.
But all the Tartar camp along the stream
Was hush'd, and still the men were plunged in sleep:
Sohrab alone, he slept not: all night long
He had lain wakeful, tossing on his bed;
But when the grey dawn stole into his tent,
He rose, and clad himself, and girt his sword,
And took his horseman's cloak, and left his tent,
And went abroad into the cold wet fog,   10
Through the dim camp to Peran-Wisa's tent.
      Through the black Tartar tents he pass'd, which stood
Clustering like bee-hives on the low flat strand
Of Oxus, where the summer floods o'erflow
When the sun melts the snows in high Pamere:
Through the black tents he pass'd, o'er that low strand,
And to a hillock came, a little back
From the stream's brink, the spot where first a boat,
Crossing the stream in summer, scrapes the land.
The men of former times had crown'd the top   20
With a clay fort: but that was fall'n; and now
The Tartars built there Peran-Wisa's tent,
A dome of laths, and o'er it felts were spread.
And Sohrab came there, and went in, and stood
Upon the thick-pil'd carpets in the tent,
And found the old man sleeping on his bed
Of rugs and felts, and near him lay his arms.
And Peran-Wisa heard him, though the step
Was dull'd; for he slept light, an old man's sleep;
And he rose quickly on one arm, and said: –   30

'Who art thou? for it is not yet clear dawn.
Speak! is there news, or any night alarm?'
   But Sohrab came to the bedside, and said: –
'Thou know'st me, Peran-Wisa: it is I.
The sun is not yet risen, and the foe
Sleep; but I sleep not; all night long I lie
Tossing and wakeful, and I come to thee.
For so did King Afrasiab bid me seek
Thy counsel, and to heed thee as thy son,
In Samarcand, before the army march'd;   40
And I will tell thee what my heart desires.
Thou knowest if, since from Ader-baijan first
I came among the Tartars, and bore arms,
I have still serv'd Afrasiab well, and shown,
At my boy's years, the courage of a man.
This too thou know'st, that, while I still bear on
The conquering Tartar ensigns through the world,
And beat the Persians back on every field,
I seek one man, one man, and one alone.
Rustum, my father; who, I hop'd, should greet,   50
Should one day greet, upon some well-fought field
His not unworthy, not inglorious son.
So I long hop'd, but him I never find.
Come then, hear now, and grant me what I ask.
Let the two armies rest to-day: but I
Will challenge forth the bravest Persian lords
To meet me, man to man: if I prevail,
Rustum will surely hear it; if I fall –
Old man, the dead need no one, claim no kin.
Dim is the rumour of a common fight,   60
Where host meets host, and many names are sunk:
But of a single combat Fame speaks clear.'
   He spoke: and Peran-Wisa took the hand
Of the young man in his, and sigh'd, and said: –
   'Oh Sohrab, an unquiet heart is thine!
Canst thou not rest among the Tartar chiefs,
And share the battle's common chance with us
Who love thee, but must press for ever first,
In single fight incurring single risk,
To find a father thou hast never seen?   70

Or, if indeed this one desire rules all,
To seek out Rustum – seek him not through fight:
Seek him in peace, and carry to his arms,
O Sohrab, carry an unwounded son!
But far hence seek him, for he is not here.
For now it is not as when I was young,
When Rustum was in front of every fray:
But now he keeps apart, and sits at home,
In Seistan, with Zal, his father old.
Whether that his own mighty strength at last   80
Feels the abhorr'd approaches of old age;
Or in some quarrel with the Persian King.
There go: – Thou wilt not? Yet my heart forebodes
Danger or death awaits thee on this field.
Fain would I know thee safe and well, though lost
To us: fain therefore send thee hence, in peace
To seek thy father, not seek single fights
In vain: – but who can keep the lion's cub
From ravening? and who govern Rustum's son?
Go: I will grant thee what thy heart desires.'   90
       So said he, and dropp'd Sohrab's hand, and left
His bed, and the warm rugs whereon he lay,
And o'er his chilly limbs his woollen coat
He pass'd, and tied his sandals on his feet,
And threw a white cloak round him, and he took
In his right hand a ruler's staff, no sword;
And on his head he plac'd his sheep-skin cap,
Black, glossy, curl'd, the fleece of Kara-Kul;
And rais'd the curtain of his tent, and call'd
His herald to his side, and went abroad.   100
       The sun, by this, had risen, and clear'd the fog
From the broad Oxus and the glittering sands:
And from their tents the Tartar horsemen fil'd
Into the open plain; so Haman bade;
Haman, who next to Peran-Wisa rul'd
The host, and still was in his lusty prime.
From their black tents, long files of horse, they stream'd:
As when, some grey November morn, the files,
In marching order spread, of long-neck'd cranes,
Stream over Casbin, and the southern slopes   110

Of Elburz, from the Aralian estuaries,
Or some frore Caspian reed-bed, southward bound
For the warm Persian sea-board: so they stream'd.
The Tartars of the Oxus, the King's guard,
First, with black sheep-skin caps and with long spears;
Large men, large steeds; who from Bokhara come
And Khiva, and ferment the milk of mares.
Next the more temperate Toorkmuns of the south,
The Tukas, and the lances of Salore,
And those from Attruck and the Caspian sands;   120
Light men, and on light steeds, who only drink
The acrid milk of camels, and their wells.
And then a swarm of wandering horse, who came
From far, and a more doubtful service own'd;
The Tartars of Ferghana, from the banks
Of the Jaxartes, men with scanty beards
And close-set skull-caps; and those wilder hordes
Who roam o'er Kipchak and the northern waste
Kalmuks and unkemp'd Kuzzaks, tribes who stray
Nearest the Pole, and wandering Kirghizzes,   130
Who come on shaggy ponies from Pamere.
These all fil'd out from camp into the plain.
And on the other side the Persians form'd:
First a light cloud of horse, Tartars they seem'd,
The Ilyats of Khorassan: and behind,
The royal troops of Persia, horse and foot,
Marshall'd battalions bright in burnished steel.
But Peran-Wisa with his herald came
Threading the Tartar squadrons to the front,
And with his staff kept back the foremost ranks.   140
And when Ferood, who led the Persians, saw
That Peran-Wisa kept the Tartars back,
He took his spear, and to the front he came,
And check'd his ranks, and fix'd them where they stood.
And the old Tartar came upon the sand
Betwixt the silent hosts, and spake, and said: –
     'Ferood, and ye, Persians and Tartars, hear!
Let there be truce between the hosts to-day.
But choose a champion from the Persian lords
To fight our champion Sohrab, man to man.'   150

As, in the country, on a morn in June,
When the dew glistens on the pearled ears,
A shiver runs through the deep corn for joy –
So, when they heard what Peran-Wisa said,
A thrill through all the Tartar squadrons ran
Of pride and hope for Sohrab, whom they lov'd.

But as a troop of pedlars, from Cabool,
Cross underneath the Indian Caucasus,
That vast sky-neighbouring mountain of milk snow;
Winding so high, that, as they mount, they pass   160
Long flocks of travelling birds dead on the snow,
Chok'd by the air, and scarce can they themselves
Slake their parch'd throats with sugar'd mulberries –
In single file they move, and stop their breath,
For fear they should dislodge the o'erhanging snows –
So the pale Persians held their breath with fear.

And to Ferood his brother Chiefs came up
To counsel: Gudurz and Zoarrah came,
And Feraburz, who rul'd the Persian host
Second, and was the uncle of the King: 170
These came and counsell'd; and then Gudurz said:
'Ferood, shame bids us take their challenge up,
Yet champion have we none to match this youth.
He has the wild stag's foot, the lion's heart.
But Rustum came last night; aloof he sits
And sullen, and has pitch'd his tents apart:
Him will I seek, and carry to his ear
The Tartar challenge, and this young man's name.
Haply he will forget his wrath, and fight.
Stand forth the while, and take their challenge up.'   180
So spake he; and Ferood stood forth and said:–
'Old man, be it agreed as thou hast said.
Let Sohrab arm, and we will find a man.'
He spoke; and Peran-Wisa turn'd, and strode
Back through the opening squadrons to his tent.
But through the anxious Persians Gudurz ran,
And cross'd the camp which lay behind, and reach'd,
Out on the sands beyond it, Rustum's tents.
Of scarlet cloth they were, and glittering gay,
Just pitch'd: the high pavilion in the midst   190

Was Rustum's, and his men lay camp'd around.
And Gudurz enter'd Rustum's tent, and found
Rustum: his morning meal was done, but still
The table stood beside him, charg'd with food;
A side of roasted sheep, and cakes of bread,
And dark green melons; and there Rustum sate
Listless, and held a falcon on his wrist,
And play'd with it; but Gudurz came and stood
Before him; and he look'd, and saw him stand;
And with a cry sprang up, and dropp'd the bird,   200
And greeted Gudurz with both hands, and said: –
'Welcome! these eyes could see no better sight.
What news? but sit down first, and eat and drink.'
    But Gudurz stood in the tent door, and said: –
'Not now: a time will come to eat and drink,
But not to-day: to-day has other needs.
The armies are drawn out, and stand at gaze:
For from the Tartars is a challenge brought
To pick a champion from the Persian lords
To fight their champion – and thou know'st his name –   210
Sohrab men call him, but his birth is hid.
O Rustum, like thy might is this young man's!
He has the wild stag's foot, the lion's heart.
And he is young, and Iran's Chiefs are old,
Or else too weak; and all eyes turn to thee.
Come down and help us, Rustum, or we lose.'
    He spoke: but Rustum answer'd with a smile: –
'Go to! if Iran's Chiefs, are old, then I
Am older: if the young are weak, the King
Errs strangely: for the King, for Kai Khosroo,   220
Himself is young, and honours younger men,
And lets the aged moulder to their graves.
Rustum he loves no more, but loves the young –
The young may rise at Sohrab's vaunts, not I.
For what care I, though all speak Sohrab's fame?
For would that I myself had such a son,
And not that one slight helpless girl I have,
A son so fam'd, so brave, to send to war,
And I to tarry with the snow-hair'd Zal,
My father, whom the robber Afghans vex,   230

And clip his borders short, and drive his herds,
And he has none to guard his weak old age.
There would I go, and hang my armour up,
And with my great name fence that weak old man,
And spend the goodly treasures I have got,
And rest my age, and hear of Sohrab's fame,
And leave to death the hosts of thankless kings,
And with these slaughterous hands draw sword no more.'
  He spoke, and smil'd; and Gudurz made reply: —
'What then, O Rustum, will men say to this,   240
When Sohrab dares our bravest forth, and seeks
Thee most of all, and thou, whom most he seeks,
Hidest thy face? Take heed, lest men should say,
Like some old miser, Rustum hoards his fame,
And shuns to peril it with younger men.'
And, greatly mov'd, then Rustum made reply: —
'O Gudurz, wherefore dost thou say such words?
Thou knowest better words than this to say.
What is one more, one less, obscure or fam'd,
Valiant or craven, young or old, to me?   250
Are not they mortal, am not I myself?
But who for men of nought would do great deeds?
Come, thou shalt see how Rustum hoards his fame.
But I will fight unknown, and in plain arms;
Let not men say of Rustum, he was match'd
In single fight with any mortal man.'
  He spoke, and frown'd; and Gudurz turn'd, and ran
Back quickly through the camp in fear and joy,
Fear at his wrath, but joy that Rustum came.
But Rustum strode to his tent door, and call'd   260
His followers in, and bade them bring his arms,
And clad himself in steel: the arms he chose
Were plain, and on his shield was no device,
Only his helm was rich, inlaid with gold,
And from the fluted spine atop a plume
Of horsehair wav'd, a scarlet horsehair plume.
So arm'd he issued forth; and Ruksh, his horse,
Follow'd him, like a faithful hound, at heel,
Ruksh, whose renown was nois'd through all the earth,
The horse, whom Rustum on a foray once   270

Did in Bokhara by the river find
A colt beneath its dam, and drove him home,
And rear'd him; a bright bay, with lofty crest;
Dight with a saddle-cloth of broider'd green
Crusted with gold, and on the ground were work'd
All beasts of chase, all beasts which hunters know:
So follow'd, Rustum left his tents, and cross'd
The camp, and to the Persian host appear'd.
And all the Persians knew him, and with shouts
Hail'd; but the Tartars knew not who he was.   280
And dear as the wet diver to the eyes
Of his pale wife who waits and weeps on shore,
By sandy Bahrein, in the Persian Gulf,
Plunging all day in the blue waves, at night,
Having made up his tale of precious pearls,
Rejoins her in their hut upon the sands –
So dear to the pale Persians Rustum came.

   And Rustum to the Persian front advan'd,
And Sohrab arm'd in Haman's tent, and came.
And as afield the reapers cut a swathe   290
Down through the middle of a rich man's corn,
And on each side are squares of standing corn,
And in the midst a stubble, short and bare;
So on each side were squares of men, with spears
Bristling, and in the midst, the open sand.
And Rustum came upon the sand, and cast
His eyes towards the Tartar tents, and saw
Sohrab come forth, and ey'd him as he came.

   As some rich woman, on a winter's morn,
Eyes through her silken curtains the poor drudge   300
Who with numb blacken'd fingers makes her fire –
At cock-crow, on a starlit winter's morn,
When the frost flowers the whiten'd window panes –
And wonders how she lives, and what the thoughts
Of that poor drudge may be; so Rustum ey'd
The unknown adventerous Youth, who from afar
Came seeking Rustum, and defying forth
All the most valiant chiefs: long he perus'd
His spirited air, and wonder'd who he was.
For very young he seem'd, tenderly rear'd;   310

Like some young cypresses, tall, and dark, and straight,
Which in a queen's secluded garden throws
Its slight dark shadow on the moonlit turf,
By midnight, to a bubbling fountain's sound –
So slender Sohrab seem'd, so softly rear'd.
And a deep pity enter'd Rustum's soul
As he beheld him coming; and he stood,
And beckon'd to him with his hand, and said: –
    'O thou young man, the air of Heaven is soft,
And warm, and pleasant; but the grave is cold.   320
Heaven's air is better than the cold dead grave.
Behold me: I am vast, and clad in iron,
And tried; and I have stood on many a field
Of blood, and I have fought with many a foe:
Never was that field lost, or that foe sav'd.
O Sohrab, wherefore wilt thou rush on death?
Be govern'd: quit the Tartar host, and come
To Iran, and be as my son to me,
And fight beneath my banner till I die.
There are no youths in Iran brave as thou.'   330
    So he spake, mildly: Sohrab heard his voice,
The mighty voice of Rustum; and he saw
His giant figure planted on the sand,
Sole, like some single tower, which a chief
Has builded on the waste in former years
Against the robbers; and he saw that head,
Streak'd with its first grey hairs: hope fill'd his soul;
And he ran fowards and embrac'd his knees,
And clasp'd his hand within his own and said: –
    'Oh, by thy father's head! by thine own soul!   340
Art thou not Rustum? Speak! art thou not he?'
    But Rustum ey'd askance the kneeling youth,
And turn'd away, and spoke to his own soul: –
    'Ah me, I muse what this young fox may mean.
False, wily, boastful, are these Tartar boys.
For if I now confess this thing he asks,
And hide it not, but say – *Rustum is here* –
He will not yield indeed, nor quit our foes,
But he will find some pretext not to fight,
And praise my fame, and proffer courteous gifts,   350

A belt or sword perhaps, and go his way.
And on a feast day, in Afrasiab's hall,
In Samarcand, he will arise and cry –
'I challeng'd once, when the two armies camp'd
Beside the Oxus, all the Persian lords
To cope with me in single fight; but they
Shrank; only Rustum dar'd: then he and I
Chang'd gifts, and went on equal terms away.'
So will he speak, perhaps, while men applaud.
Then were the chiefs of Iran sham'd through me.'   360

   And then he turn'd, and sternly spake aloud: –
'Rise! wherefore dost thou vainly questions thus
Of Rustum? I am here, whom thou hast call'd
By challenge forth: make good thy vaunt, or yield.
Is it with Rustum only thou wouldst fight?
Rash boy, men look on Rustum's face and flee.
For well I know, that did great Rustum stand
Before thy face this day, and were reveal'd,
There would be then no talk of fighting more.
But being what I am, I tell thee this;   370
Do thou record it in thine inmost soul:
Either thou shalt renounce thy vaunt, and yield;
Or else thy bones shall strew this sand, till winds
Bleach them, or Oxus with his summer floods,
Oxus in summer wash them all away.'

   He spoke: and Sohrab answer'd, on his feet: –
'Art thou so fierce? Thou wilt not fright me so.
I am no girl, to be made pale by words.
Yet this thou hast said well, did Rustum stand
Here on this field, there were no fighting then.   380
But Rustum is far hence, and we stand here.
Begin: thou art more vast, more dread than I,
And thou art prov'd, I know, and I am young –
But yet Success sways with the breath of Heaven.
And though thou thinkest that thou knowest sure
Thy victory, yet thou canst not surely know.
For we are all, like swimmers in the sea,
Pois'd on the top of a huge wave of Fate,
Which hangs uncertain to which side to fall.
And whether it will heave us up to land,   390

Or whether it will roll us out to sea,
Back out to sea, to the deep waves of death,
We know not, and no search will make us know:
Only the event will teach us in its hour.'

  He spoke; and Rustum answer'd not, but hurl'd
His spear: down from the shoulder, down it came,
As on some partridge in the corn a hawk
That long has tower'd in the airy clouds
Drops like a plummet: Sohrab saw it come,
And sprang aside, quick as a flash: the spear   400
Hiss'd, and went quivering down into the sand,
Which it sent flying wide: – then Sohrab threw
In turn, and full struck Rustum's shield: sharp rang,
The iron plates rang sharp, but turn'd the spear.
And Rustum seiz'd his club, which none but he
Could wield: an unlopp'd trunk it was, and huge,
Still rough; like those which men in treeless plains
To build them boats fish from the flooded rivers,
Hyphasis or Hydaspes, when, high up
By their dark springs, the wind in winter-time   410
Has made in Himalayan forests wrack,
And strewn the channels with torn boughs; so huge
The club which Rustum lifted now, and struck
One stroke; but again Sohrab sprang aside
Lithe as the glancing snake, and the club came
Thundering to earth, and leapt from Rustum's hand.
And Rustum follow'd his own blow, and fell
To his knees, and with his fingers clutch'd the sand
And now might Sohrab have unsheath'd his sword,
And pierc'd the mighty Rustum while he lay   420
Dizzy, and on his knees, and chok'd with sand:
But he look'd on, and smil'd, nor bar'd his sword,
But courteously drew back, and spoke, and said:–

  'Thou strik'st too hard: that club of thine will float
Upon the summer floods, and not my bones.
But rise, and be not wroth; not wroth am I:
No, when I see thee, wrath forsakes my soul.
Thou say'st, thou art not Rustum: be it so.
Who art thou then, that canst so touch my soul?
Boy as I am, I have seen battles too;   430

Have waded foremost in their bloody waves,
And heard their hollow roar of dying men;
But never was my heart thus touch'd before.
Are they from Heaven, these softenings of the heart?
O thou old warrior, let us yield to Heaven!
Come, plant we here in earth our angry spears,
And make a truce, and sit upon this sand,
And pledge each other in red wine, like friends,
And thou shalt talk to me of Rustum's deeds.
There are enough foes in the Persian host   440
Whom I may meet, and strike, and feel no pang;
Champions enough Afrasiab has, whom thou
Mayst fight; fight them, when they confront thy spear.
But oh, let there be peace 'twixt thee and me!'

   He ceas'd: but while he spake, Rustum had risen
And stood erect, trembling with rage: his club
He left to lie, but had regain'd his spear,
Whose fiery point now in his mail'd right-hand
Blaz'd bright and baleful, like that autumn Star,
The baleful sign of fevers: dust had soil'd   450
His stately crest, and dimm'd his glittering arms.
His breast heav'd; his lips foam'd; and twice his voice
Was chok'd with rage: at last these words broke way:–
   'Girl! nimble with thy feet, not with thy hands!
Curl'd minion, dancer, coiner of sweet words!
Fight; let me hear thy hateful voice no more!
Thou art not in Afrasiab's gardens now
With Tartar girls, with whom thou art wont to dance
But on the Oxus sands, and in the dance
Of battle, and with me, who make no play   460
Of war: I fight it out, and hand to hand.
Speak not to me of truce, and pledge, and wine!
Remember all thy valour: try thy feints
And cunning: all the pity I had is gone:
Because thou hast sham'd me before both the hosts
With thy light skipping tricks, and thy girl's wiles.'
   He spoke; and Sohrab kindled at his taunts,
And he too drew his sword: at once they rush'd
Together, as two eagles on one prey

Come rushing down together from the clouds,   470
One from the east, one from the west: their shields
Dash'd with a clang together, and a din
Rose, such as that the sinewy woodcutters
Make often in the forest's heart at morn,
Of hewing axes, crashing trees: such blows
Rustum and Sohrab on each other hail'd.
And you would say that sun and stars took part
In that unnatural conflict; for a cloud
Grew suddenly in Heaven, and dark'd the sun
Over the fighters' heads; and a wind rose   480
Under their feet, and moaning swept the plain,
And in a sandy whirlwind wrapp'd the pair.
In gloom they twain were wrapp'd, and they alone;
For both the on-looking hosts on either hand
Stood in broad daylight, and the sky was pure,
And the sun sparkled on the Oxus stream.
But in the gloom they fought, with bloodshot eyes
And laboured breath; first Rustum struck the shield
Which Sohrab held stiff out: the steel-spik'd spear
Rent the tough plates, but fail'd to reach the skin,   490
And Rustum pluck'd it back with angry groan.
Then Sohrab with his sword smote Rustum's helm,
Nor clove its steel quite through; but all the crest
He shore away, and that proud horsehair plume,
Never till now defil'd, sunk to the dust;
And Rustum bow'd his head; but then the gloom
Grew blacker: thunder rumbled in the air,
And lightnings rent the cloud; and Ruksh, the horse
Who stood at hand, utter'd a dreadful cry:
No horse's cry was that, most like the roar   500
Of some pain'd desert lion, who all day
Has trail'd the hunter's javelin in his side,
And comes at night to die upon the sand:—
The two hosts heard that cry, and quak'd for fear,
And Oxus curdled as it cross'd his stream.
But Sohrab heard, and quail'd not, but rush'd on,
And struck again; and again Rustum bow'd
His head; but this time all the blade, like glass,
Sprang in a thousand shivers on the helm,

And in his hand the hilt remain'd alone. 510
Then Rustum rais'd his head: his dreadful eyes
Glar'd, and he shook on high his menacing spear,
And shouted, *Rustum!* Sohrab heard that shout,
And shrank amaz'd: back he recoil'd one step,
And scann'd with blinking eyes the advancing Form:
And then he stood bewilder'd; and he dropp'd
His covering shield, and the spear pierc'd his side.
He reel'd, and staggering back, sunk to the ground.
And then the gloom dispers'd, and the wind fell,
And the bright sun broke forth, and melted all 520
The cloud; and the two armies saw the pair;
Saw Rustum standing, safe upon his feet,
And Sohrab, wounded, on the bloody sand.
    Then, with a bitter smile, Rustum began:–
'Sohrab, thou thoughtest in thy mind to kill
A Persian lord this day, and strip his corpse,
And bear thy trophies to Afrasiab's tent.
Or else that the great Rustum would come down
Himself to fight, and that thy wiles would move
His heart to take a gift, and let thee go. 530
And then that all the Tartar host would praise
Thy courage or thy craft, and spread thy fame,
To glad thy father in his weak old age.
Fool! thou art slain, and by an unknown man!
Dearer to the red jackals shalt thou be,
Than to thy friends, and to thy father old.'
    And, with a fearless mien, Sohrab replied:–
'Unknown thou art; yet thy fierce vaunt is vain.
Thou dost not slay me, proud and boastful man!
No! Rustum slays me, and this filial heart. 540
For were I match'd with ten such men as thou,
And I were he who still to-day I was,
They should be lying here, I standing there.
But that beloved name unnerv'd my arm –
That name, and something, I confess, in thee,
Which troubles all my heart, and made my shield
Fall; and thy spear transfix'd an unarm'd foe.
And now thou boastest, and insult'st my fate.
But hear thou this, fierce Man, tremble to hear!

The mighty Rustum shall avenge my death!   550
My father, whom I seek through all the world,
He shall avenge my death, and punish thee!'
    As when some hunter in the spring hath found
A breeding eagle sitting on her nest,
Upon the craggy isle of a hill lake,
And pierc'd her with an arrow as she rose,
And follow'd her to find her where she fell
Far off; – anon her mate comes winging back
From hunting, and a great way off descries
His huddling young left sole; at that, he checks   560
His pinion, and with short uneasy sweeps
Circles above his eyry, with loud screams
Chiding his mate back to her nest; but she
Lies dying, with the arrow in her side,
In some far stony gorge out of his ken,
A heap of fluttering feathers: never more
Shall the lake glass her, flying over it;
Never the black and dripping precipices
Echo her stormy scream as she sails by:–
As that poor bird flies home, nor knows his loss –   570
So Rustum knew not his own loss, but stood
Over his dying son, and knew him not.
    But with a cold, incredulous voice, he said: –
'What prate is this of fathers and revenge?
The mighty Rustum never had a son.'
    And, with a failing voice, Sohrab replied:–
'Ah yes, he had! and that lost son am I.
Surely the news will one day reach his ear,
Reach Rustum, where he sits, and tarries long,
Somewhere, I know not where, but far from here;   580
And pierce him like a stab, and make him leap
To arms, and cry for vengeance upon thee.
Fierce Man, bethink thee, for an only son!
What will that grief, what will that vengeance be!
Oh, could I live, till I that grief had seen!
Yet him I pity not so much, but her,
My mother, who in Ader-baijan dwells
With that old King, her father, who grows grey
With age, and rules over the valiant Koords.

Her most I pity, who no more will see   590
Sohrab returning from the Tartar camp,
With spoils and honour, when the war is done.
But a dark rumour will be bruited up,
From tribe to tribe, until it reach her ear;
And then will that defenceless woman learn
That Sohrab will rejoice her sight no more;
But that in battle with a nameless foe,
By the far distant Oxus, he is slain.'
　　He spoke; and as he ceas'd he wept aloud,
Thinking of her he left, and his own death.   600
He spoke; but Rustum listen'd, plung'd in thought.
Nor did he yet believe it was his son
Who spoke, although he call'd back names he knew;
For he had had sure tidings that the babe,
Which was in Ader-baijan born to him,
Had been a puny girl, no boy at all:
So that sad mother sent him word, for fear
Rustum should take the boy, to train in arms;
And so he deem'd that either Sohrab took,
By a false boast, the style of Rustum's son;   610
Or that men gave it him, to swell his fame.
So deem'd he; yet he listen'd, plung'd in thought;
And his soul set to grief, as the vast tide
Of the bright rocking Ocean sets to shore
At the full moon: tears gathered in his eyes;
For he remember'd his own early youth,
And all its bounding rapture; as, at dawn,
The Shepherd from his mountain lodge descries
A far bright City, smitten by the sun,
Through many rolling clouds; – so Rustum saw   620
His youth; saw Sohrab's mother, in her bloom;
And that old King, her father, who lov'd well
His wandering guest, and gave him his fair child
With joy; and all the pleasant life they led,
They three, in that long-distant summer-time –
The castle, and the dewy woods, and hunt
And hound, and morn on those delightful hills
In Ader-baijan. And he saw that Youth,
Of age and looks to be his own dear son,

Piteous and lovely, lying on the sand,   630
Like some rich hyacinth, which by the scythe
Of an unskilful gardener has been cut,
Mowing the garden grass-plots near its bed,
And lies, a fragrant tower of purple bloom,
On the mown, dying grass; – so Sohrab lay,
Lovely in death, upon the common sand.
And Rustum gaz'd on him with grief, and said: –
    'O Sohrab, thou indeed art such a son
Whom Rustum, wert thou his, might well have lov'd!
Yet here thou errest, Sohrab, or else men   640
Have told thee false; – thou art not Rustum's son.
For Rustum had no son: one child he had –
But one – a girl: who with her mother now
Plies some light female task, nor dreams of us –
Of us she dreams not, nor of wounds, nor war.'
    But Sohrab answer'd him in wrath; for now
The anguish of the deep-fix'd spear grew fierce,
And he desired to draw forth the steel,
And let the blood flow free, and so to die;
But first he would convince his stubborn foe –   650
And, rising sternly on one arm, he said:–
    'Man, who art thou who dost deny my words?
Truth sits upon the lips of dying men,
And Falsehood, while I liv'd, was far from mine.
I tell thee, prick'd upon this arm I bear
That seal which Rustum to my mother gave,
That she might prick it on the babe she bore.'
    He spoke: and all the blood left Rustum's cheeks;
And his knees totter'd, and he smote his hand,
Against his breast, his heavy mailed hand,   660
That the hard iron corslet clank'd aloud:
And to his heart he press'd the other hand,
And in a hollow voice he spake, and said: –
    'Sohrab, that were a proof which could not lie.
If thou shew this, then art thou Rustum's son.'
    Then, with weak hasty fingers, Sohrab loos'd
His belt, and near the shoulder bar'd his arm,
And shew'd a sign in faint vermilion points
Prick'd: as a cunning workman, in Pekin,

Pricks with vermilion some clear porcelain vase,   670
An emperor's gift – at early morn he paints,
And all day long, and, when night comes, the lamp
Lights up his studious forehead and thin hands: –
So delicately prick'd the sign appear'd
On Sohrab's arm, the sign of Rustum's seal.
It was that Griffin, which of old rear'd Zal,
Rustum's great father, whom they left to die,
A helpless babe, among the mountain rocks.
Him that kind Creature found, and rear'd, and lov'd –
Then Rustum took it for his glorious sign.   680
And Sohrab bar'd that figure on his arm,
And himself scann'd it long with mournful eyes,
And then he touch'd it with his hand and said:–
   'How say'st thou? Is that sign the proper sign
Of Rustum's son, or of some other man's?'
   He spoke: but Rustum gaz'd, and gaz'd, and stood
Speechless; and then he utter'd one sharp cry –
O Boy – thy Father! – and his voice chok'd there.
And then a dark cloud pass'd before his eyes,
And his head swam, and he sunk down to earth.   690
But Sohrab crawl'd to where he lay, and cast
His arms about his neck, and kiss'd his lips,
And with fond faltering fingers strok'd his cheeks,
Trying to call him back to life: and life
Came back to Rustum, and he op'd his eyes,
And they stood wide with horror; and he seiz'd
In both his hands the dust which lay around,
And threw it on his head, and smirch'd his hair,
His hair, and face, and beard, and glittering arms:
And strong convulsive groanings shook his breast,   700
And his sobs chok'd him; and he clutch'd his sword,
To draw it, and for ever let life out.
But Sohrab saw his thought, and held his hands,
And with a soothing voice he spoke, and said:–
'Father, forbear: for I but meet to-day
The doom that at my birth was written down
In Heaven, and thou art Heaven's unconscious hand.
Surely my heart cried out that it was thou,
When first I saw thee; and thy heart spoke too,

I know it: but Fate trod those promptings down   710
Under its iron heel; Fate, Fate engag'd
The strife, and hurl'd me on my father's spear.
But let us speak no more of this: I find
My father; let me feel that I have found.
Come, sit beside me on this sand, and take
My head betwixt thy hands, and kiss my cheeks,
And wash them with thy tears, and say, 'My Son!'
Quick! quick! for number'd are my sands of life,
And swift; for like the lightning to this field
I came, and like the wind I go away –   720
Sudden, and swift, and like a passing wind.
But it was writ in Heaven that this should be.'
    So said he: and his voice releas'd the heart
Of Rustum, and his tears broke forth; he cast
His arms round his son's neck, and wept aloud,
And kiss'd him. And awe fell on both the hosts
When they saw Rustum's grief: and Ruksh, the horse,
With his head bowing to the ground, and mane
Sweeping the dust, came near, and in mute woe
First to the one then to the other mov'd   730
His head, as if enquiring what their grief
Might mean; and from his dark, compassionate eyes
The big warm tears roll'd down, and cak'd the sand.
But Rustum chid him with stern voice, and said:–
    'Ruksh, now thou grievest; but, O Ruksh, thy feet
Should then have rotted on thy nimble joints,
When first they bore thy Master to this field.'
    But Sohrab look'd upon the horse and said:–
'Is this then Ruksh? How often, in past days,
My mother told me of thee, thou brave Steed!   740
My terrible father's terrible horse; and said,
That I should one day find thy lord and thee.
Come, let me lay my hand upon thy mane.
O Ruksh, thou art more fortunate than I;
For thou hast gone where I shall never go,
And snuff'd the breezes of my father's home.
And thou hast trod the sands of Seistan,
And seen the River of Helmund, and the Lake
Of Zirrah; and the aged Zal himself

Has often strok'd thy neck, and given thee food,   750
Corn in a golden platter soak'd with wine,
And said – "O Ruksh! bear Rustum well!" – but I
Have never known my grandsire's furrow'd face,
Nor seen his lofty house in Seistan,
Nor slak'd my thirst at the clear Helmund stream:
But lodg'd among my father's foes, and seen
Afrasiab's cities only, Samarcand,
Bokhara, and lone Khiva in the waste,
And the black Toorkmun tents; and only drunk
The desert rivers, Moorghab and Tejend,   760
Kohik, and where the Kalmuks feed their sheep,
The northern Sir; and this great Oxus stream –
The yellow Oxus, by whose brink I die.'
   And, with a heavy groan, Rustum replied:–
'Oh that its waves were flowing over me!
Oh that I saw its grains of yellow silt
Roll tumbling in the current o'er my head!'
   And, with a grave mild voice, Sohrab replied:–
'Desire not that, my father; thou must live.
For some are born to do great deeds, and live,   770
As some are born to be obscur'd, and die.
Do thou the deeds I die to young to do,
And reap a second glory in thine age.
Thou art my father, and thy gain is mine.
But come: thou seest this great host of men
Which follow me; I pray thee, slay not these:
Let me entreat for them: what have they done?
They follow'd me, my hope, my fame, my star.
Let them all cross the Oxus back in peace.
But me thou must bear hence, not send with them,   780
But carry me with thee to Seistan,
And place me on a bed, and mourn for me,
Thou, and the snow-hair'd Zal, and all thy friends
And thou must lay me in that lovely earth,
And heap a stately mound above my bones,
And plant a far-seen pillar over all:
That so the passing horseman on the waste
May see my tomb a great way off, and say –
Sohrab, the mighty Rustum's son, lies there,

Whom his great father did in ignorance kill –   790
And I be not forgotten in my grave.'
    And, with a mournful voice, Rustum replied:–
'Fear not; as thou hast said, Sohrab, my son,
So shall it be: for I will burn my tents,
And quit the host, and bear thee hence with me,
And carry thee away to Seistan,
And place thee on a bed, and mourn for thee,
With the snow-headed Zal, and all my friends.
And I will lay thee in that lovely earth,
And heap a stately mound above thy bones,   800
And plant a far-seen pillar over all:
And men shall not forget thee in thy grave.
And I will spare thy host: yea, let them go:
Let them all cross the Oxus back in peace.
What should I do with slaying any more?
For would that all whom I have ever slain
Might be once more alive; my bitterest foes,
And they who were call'd champions in their time,
And through whose death I won that fame I have;
And I were nothing but a common man,   810
A poor, mean soldier, and without renown;
So thou mightest live too, my Son, my Son!
Or rather would that I, even I myself,
Might now be lying on this bloody sand,
Near death, and by an ignorant stroke of thine,
Not thou of mine; and I might die, not thou;
And I, not thou, be borne to Seistan;
And Zal might weep above my grave, not thine;
And say – *O son, I weep thee not too sore,*
For willingly, I know, thou met'st thine end. –   820
But now in blood and battles was my youth,
And full of blood and battles is my age;
And I shall never end this life of blood.'
    Then, at the point of death, Sohrab replied: –
'A life of blood indeed, thou dreadful Man!
But thou shalt yet have peace; only not now;
Not yet: but thou shalt have it on that day,
When thou shalt sail in a high-masted Ship,
Thou and the other peers of Kai-Khosroo,

Returning home over the salt blue sea, 830
From laying thy dear Master in his grave.'
  And Rustum gaz'd on Sohrab's face, and said: –
'Soon be that day, my Son, and deep that sea!
Till then, if Fate so wills, let me endure.'
  He spoke; and Sohrab smil'd on him, and took
The spear, and drew it from his side, and eas'd
His wound's imperious anguish: but the blood
Came welling from the open gash, and life
Flow'd with the stream: all down his cold white side
The crimson torrent pour'd, dim now, and soil'd, 840
Like the soil'd tissue of white violets
Left, freshly gather'd, on their native bank,
By romping children, whom their nurses call
From the hot fields at noon: his head droop'd low,
His limbs grew slack; motionless, white, he lay –
White, with eyes clos'd; only when heavy gasps,
Deep, heavy gasps, quivering through all his frame,
Convuls'd him back to life, he open'd them,
And fix'd them feebly on his father's face:
Till now all strength was ebb'd, and from his limbs 850
Unwillingly the spirit fled away,
Regretting the warm mansion which it left,
And youth and bloom, and this delightful world.
  So, on the bloody sand, Sohrab lay dead.
And the great Rustum drew his horseman's cloak
Down o'er his face, and sate by his dead son.
As those black granite pillars, once high-rear'd
By Jemshid in Persepolis, to bear
His house, now, mid their broken flights of steps,
Lie prone, enormous, down the mountain side – 860
So in the sand lay Rustum by his son.
  And night came down over the solemn waste,
And the two gazing hosts, and that sole pair,
And darken'd all; and a cold fog, with night,
Crept from the Oxus. Soon a hum arose,
As of a great assembly loos'd, and fires
Began to twinkle through the fog: for now
Both armies mov'd to camp, and took their meal:
The Persians took it on the open sands

Southward; the Tartars by the river marge: 870
And Rustum and his son were left alone.
   But the majestic River floated on,
Out of the mist and hum of that low land,
Into the frosty starlight, and there mov'd,
Rejoicing, through the hush'd Chorasmian waste,
Under the solitary moon: he flow'd
Right for the Polar Star, past Orgunjè,
Brimming, and bright, and large: then sands begin
To hem his watery march, and dam his streams,
And split his currents; that for many a league   880
The shorn and parcell'd Oxus strains along
Through beds of sand and matted rushy isles –
Oxus, forgetting the bright speed he had
In his high mountain cradle in Pamere,
A foil'd circuitous wanderer: – till at last
The long'd-for dash of waves is heard, and wide
His luminous home of waters opens, bright
And tranquil, from whose floor the new-bath'd stars
Emerge, and shine upon the Aral Sea.

Cadmus and Harmonia

        Far, far, from here,
The Adriatic breaks in a warm bay
Among the green Illyrian hills; and there
The sunshine in the happy glens is fair,
And by the sea, and in the brakes.
The grass is cool, the sea-side air
Buoyant and fresh, the mountain flowers
More virginal and sweet than ours.
And there, they say, two bright and aged Snakes,
Who once were Cadmus and Harmonia,   10
Bask in the glens or on the warm sea-shore,
In breathless quiet, after all their ills.
Nor do they see their country, nor the place

Where the Sphinx liv'd among the frowning hills,
Nor the unhappy palace of their race,
Nor Thebes, nor the Ismenus, any more.

There those two live, far in the Illyrian brakes.
They had stay'd long enough to see,
In Thebes, the billow of calamity
Over their own dear children roll'd,   20
Curse upon curse, pang upon pang,
For years, they sitting helpless in their home,
A grey old man and woman: yet of old
The Gods had to their marriage come,
And at the banquet all the Muses sang.

Therefore they did not end their days
In sight of blood; but were rapt, far away,
To where the west wind plays,
And murmurs of the Adriatic come
To those untrodden mountain lawns: and there   30
Placed safely in chang'd forms, the Pair
Wholly forget their first sad life, and home,
And all that Theban woe, and stray
For ever through the glens, placid and dumb.

The Scholar Gipsy

Go, for they call you, Shepherd, from the hill;
  Go, Shepherd, and untie the wattled cotes:
    No longer leave thy wistful flock unfed,
  Nor let thy bawling fellows rack their throats,
    Nor the cropp'd grasses shoot another head.
      But when the fields are still,
  And the tired men and dogs all gone to rest,
    And only the white sheep are sometimes seen
    Cross and recross the strips of moon-blanch'd green;
      Come, Shepherd, and again renew the quest.   10

Here, where the reaper was at work of late,
   In this high field's dark corner, where he leaves
     His coat, his basket, and his earthen cruise,
  And in the sun all morning binds the sheaves,
     Then here, at noon, comes back his stores to use;
      Here will I sit and wait,
  While to my ear from uplands far away
     The bleating of the folded flocks is borne;
     With distant cries of reapers in the corn –
      All the live murmur of a summer's day.   20

Screen'd is this nook o'er the high, half-reap'd field,
   And here till sun-down, Shepherd, will I be.
     Through the thick corn the scarlet poppies peep
  And round green roots and yellowing stalks I see
     Pale blue convolvulus in tendrils creep:
      And air-swept lindens yield
  Their scent, and rustle down their perfum'd showers
     Of bloom on the bent grass where I am laid,
     And bower me from the August sun with shade;
      And the eye travels down to Oxford's towers: 30

And near me on the grass lies Glanvil's book –
   Come, let me read the oft-read tale again,
     The story of that Oxford scholar poor
  Of pregnant parts and quick inventive brain,
     Who, tir'd of knocking at Preferment's door,
      One summer morn forsook
  His friends, and went to learn the Gipsy lore,
     And roam'd the world with that wild brotherhood,
     And came, as most men deem'd, to little good,
      But came to Oxford and his friends no more.   40

But once, years after, in the country lanes,
   Two scholars whom at college erst he knew
     Met him, and of his way of life enquir'd.
  Whereat he answer'd, that the Gipsy crew,
     His mates, had arts to rule as they desir'd
      The workings of men's brains;
      And they can bind them to what thoughts they will

'And I,' he said, 'the secret of their art,
When fully learn'd, will to the world impart:
But it needs happy moments for this skill.'   50

This said, he left them and return'd no more,
But rumours hung about the country side
That the lost Scholar long was seen to stray,
Seen by rare glimpses, pensive and tongue-tied,
In hat of antique shape, and cloak of grey,
The same the Gipsies wore.
Shepherds had met him on the Hurst in spring:
At some lone alehouse in the Berkshire moors,
On the warm ingle bench, the smock-frock'd boors
Had found him seated at their entering,   60

But, mid their drink and clatter, he would fly:
And I myself seem half to know thy looks,
And put the shepherds, Wanderer, on thy trace;
And boys who in lone wheatfields scare the rooks
I ask if thou hast pass'd their quiet place;
Or in my boat I lie
Moor'd to the cool bank in the summer heats,
Mid wide grass meadows which the sunshine fills,
And watch the warm green-muffled Cumner hills,
And wonder if thou haunt'st their shy retreats.   70

For most, I know, thou lov'st retired ground.
Thee, at the ferry, Oxford riders blithe,
Returning home on summer nights, have met
Crossing the stripling Thames at Bab-lock-hithe,
Trailing in the cool stream thy fingers wet,
As the slow punt swings round:
And leaning backwards in a pensive dream,
And fostering in thy lap a heap of flowers
Pluck'd in shy fields and distant woodland bowers,
And thine eyes resting on the moonlit stream   80

And then they land, and thou art seen no more.
Maidens who from the distant hamlets come
To dance around the Fyfield elm in May,

Oft through the darkening fields have seen thee roam,
　Or cross a stile into the public way.
　　Oft thou hast given them store
Of flowers – the frail-leaf'd, white anemone –
　Dark bluebells drench'd with dews of summer eves –
　And purple orchises with spotted leaves –
　　But none has words she can report of thee.　　90

And, above Godstow Bridge, when hay-time's here
　In June, and many a scythe in sunshine flames,
　　Men who through those wide fields of breezy grass
Where black-wing'd swallows haunt the glittering Thames,
　To bathe in the abandon'd lasher pass,
　　Have often pass'd thee near
Sitting upon the river bank o'ergrown:
　Mark'd thy outlandish garb, thy figure spare,
　Thy dark vague eyes, and soft abstracted air;
　　But, when they came from bathing, thou wert gone.　　100

At some lone homestead in the Cumner hills,
　Where at her open door the housewife darns,
　　Thou hast been seen, or hanging on a gate
To watch the threshers in the mossy barns.
　Children, who early range these slopes and late
　　For cresses from the rills,
Have known thee watching, all an April day,
　The springing pastures and the feeding kine;
　And mark'd thee, when the stars come out and shine,
　　Through the long dewy grass move slow away.　　110

In Autumn, on the skirts of Bagley wood,
　Where most the Gipsies by the turf-edg'd way
　　Pitch their smok'd tents, and every bush you see
With scarlet patches tagg'd and shreds of grey,
　Above the forest ground call'd Thessaly –
　　The blackbird picking food
Sees thee, nor stops his meal, nor fears at all;
　So often has he known thee past him stray
　Rapt, twirling in thy hand a wither'd spray,
　　And waiting for the spark from Heaven to fall.　　120

And once, in winter, on the causeway chill
    Where home through flooded fields foot-travellers go,
        Have I not pass'd thee on the wooden bridge
    Wrapt in thy cloak and battling with the snow,
        Thy face towards Hinksey and its wintry ridge?
            And thou hast climb'd the hill
    And gain'd the white brow of the Cumner range,
        Turn'd once to watch, while thick the snow-flakes fall,
    The line of festal light in Christ-Church hall –
        Then sought thy straw in some sequester'd grange.   130

But what – I dream! Two hundred years are flown
    Since first thy story ran through Oxford halls,
        And the grave Glanvil did the tale inscribe
    That thou wert wander'd from the studious walls
        To learn strange arts, and join a Gipsy tribe:
            And thou from earth art gone
    Long since, and in some quiet churchyard laid;
        Some country nook, where o'er thy unknown grave
        Tall grasses and white flowering nettles wave –
        Under a dark red-fruited yew-tree's shade.   140

– No, no, thou hast not felt the lapse of hours.
    For what wears out the life of mortal men?
        'Tis that from change to change their being rolls:
        'Tis that repeated shocks, again, again,
        Exhaust the energy of strongest souls,
            And numb the elastic powers.
    Till having us'd our nerves with bliss and teen,
        And tir'd upon a thousand schemes our wit,
        To the just-pausing Genius we remit
        Our worn-out life, and are – what we have been.   150

Thou hast not liv'd, why should'st thou perish, so?
    Thou hadst *one* aim, *one* business, *one* desire:
        Else wert thou long since number'd with the dead –
    Else hadst thou spent, like other men, thy fire.
        The generations of thy peers are fled,
            And we ourselves shall go;
    But thou possessest an immortal lot,

And we imagine thee exempt from age
And living as thou liv'st on Glanvil's page,
   Because thou hadst – what we, alas, have not!   160

For early didst thou leave the world, with powers
   Fresh, undiverted to the world without,
      Firm to their mark, not spent on other things:
   Free from the sick fatigue, the languid doubt,
      Which much to have tried, in much been baffled, brings.
         O Life unlike to ours!
   Who fluctuate idly without term or scope,
      Of whom each strives, nor knows for what he strives,
      And each half lives a hundred different lives;
         Who wait like thee, but not, like thee, in hope.   170

Thou waitest for the spark from Heaven: and we,
   Light half-believers of our casual creeds,
      Who never deeply felt, nor clearly will'd,
   Whose insight never has borne fruit in deeds,
      Whose vague resolves never have been fulfill'd:
         For whom each year we see
   Breeds new beginnings, disappointments new;
      Who hesitate and falter life away,
      And lose to-morrow the ground won to-day –
         Ah, do not we, Wanderer, await it too?   180

Yes, we await it, but it still delays,
   And then we suffer; and amongst us One,
      Who most has suffer'd, takes dejectedly
   His seat upon the intellectual throne;
      And all his store of sad experience he
         Lays bare of wretched days;
   Tells us his misery's birth and growth and signs,
      And how the dying spark of hope was fed,
      And how the breast was sooth'd, and how the head,
         And all his hourly varied anodynes.   190

This for our wisest: and we others pine,
   And wish the long unhappy dream would end,
      And waive all claim to bliss, and try to bear

With close-lipp'd Patience for our only friend,
 Sad Patience, too near neighbour to Despair:
 But none has hope like thine.
Thou through the fields and through the woods dost stray,
 Roaming the country side, a truant boy,
 Nursing thy project in unclouded joy,
  And every doubt long blown by time away.   200

O born in days when wits were fresh and clear,
 And life ran gaily as the sparkling Thames;
  Before this strange disease of modern life,
 With its sick hurry, its divided aims,
  Its heads o'ertax'd, its palsied hearts, was rife –
   Fly hence, our contact fear!
 Still fly, plunge deeper in the bowering wood!
  Averse, as Dido did with gesture stern
  From her false friend's approach in Hades turn,
   Wave us away, and keep thy solitude.   210

Still nursing the unconquerable hope,
 Still clutching the inviolable shade,
  With a free onward impulse brushing through,
 By night, the silver'd branches of the glade –
  Far on the forest skirts, where none pursue,
   On some mild pastoral slope
 Emerge, and resting on the moonlit pales,
  Freshen thy flowers, as in former years,
  With dew, or listen with enchanted ears,
   From the dark dingles, to the nightingales.   220

But fly our paths, our feverish contact fly!
 For strong the infection of our mental strife,
  Which, though it gives no bliss, yet spoils for rest;
 And we should win thee from thy own fair life,
  Like us distracted, and like us unblest.
   Soon, soon thy cheer would die,
 Thy hopes grow timorous, and unfix'd thy powers,
  And thy clear aims be cross and shifting made:
  And then thy glad perennial youth would fade,
   Fade, and grow old at last and die like ours.   230

Then fly our greetings, fly our speech and smiles!
  – And some grave Tyrian trader, from the sea,
    Descried at sunrise an emerging prow
Lifting the cool-hair'd creepers stealthily,
    The fringes of a southward-facing brow
      Among the Ægean isles;
And saw the merry Grecian coaster come,
    Freighted with amber grapes, and Chian wine,
    Green bursting figs, and tunnies steep'd in brine;
      And knew the intruders on his ancient home,   240

The young light-hearted Masters of the waves;
    And snatch'd his rudder, and shook out more sail,
    And day and night held on indignantly
O'er the blue Midland waters with the gale,
    Betwixt the Syrtes and soft Sicily,
      To where the Atlantic raves
Outside the Western Straits, and unbent sails
    There, where down cloudy cliffs, through sheets of foam,
    Shy traffickers, the dark Iberians come;
      And on the beach undid his corded bales.   250

from **Poems, Second Series** (1855)

The Harp-Player on Etna

THE LAST GLEN

The track winds down to the clear stream,
To cross the sparkling shallows: there
The cattle love to gather, on their way
To the high mountain pastures, and to stay,
Till the rough cow-herds drive them past,
Knee-deep in the cool ford: for 'tis the last
Of all the woody, high, well-water'd dells
On Etna; and the beam
Of noon is broken there by chestnut boughs
Down its steep verdant sides: the air   10
Is freshen'd by the leaping stream, which throws
Eternal showers of spray on the moss'd roots
Of trees, and veins of turf, and long dark shoots
Of ivy-plants, and fragrant hanging bells
Of hyacinths, and on late anemones,
That muffle its wet banks: but glade,
And stream, and sward, and chestnut trees,
End here: Etna beyond, in the broad glare
Of the hot noon, without a shade,
Slope behind slope, up to the peak, lies bare;   20
The peak, round which the white clouds play.

In such a glen, on such a day,
On Pelion, on the grassy ground,
Chiron, the aged Centaur, lay;
The young Achilles standing by.
The Centaur taught him to explore
The mountains: where the glens are dry,
And the tir'd Centaurs come to rest,

And where the soaking springs abound,
And the straight ashes grow for spears,   30
And where the hill-goats come to feed,
And the sea-eagles build their nest.
He show'd him Phthia far away,
And said – *O Boy, I taught this lore*
To Peleus, in long-distant years. –
He told him of the Gods, the stars,
The tides: – and then of mortal wars,
And of the life that Heroes lead
Before they reach the Elysian place
And rest in the immortal mead: 40
    And all the wisdom of his race.

II

TYPHO

The lyre's voice is lovely everywhere.
In the court of Gods, in the city of men,
And in the lonely rock-strewn mountain glen,
In the still mountain air.

    Only to Typho it sounds hatefully,
Only to Typho, the rebel o'erthrown,
Through whose heart Etna drives her roots of stone,
To imbed them in the sea.

    Wherefore dost thou groan so loud?
Wherefore do thy nostrils flash,   10
Through the dark night, suddenly,
Typho, such red jets of flame?
Is thy tortur'd heart still proud?
Is thy fire-scath'd arm still rash?
Still alert thy stone-crush'd frame?

    Does thy fierce soul still deplore
Thy ancient rout in the Cilician hills,
And that curst treachery on the Mount of Gore?
    Do thy bloodshot eyes still see
The fight that crown'd thy ills,   20

Thy last defeat in this Sicilian sea?
Hast thou sworn, in thy sad lair,
Where erst the strong sea-currents suck'd thee down
Never to cease to writhe, and try to sleep,
Letting the sea-stream wander through thy hair?
That thy groans, like thunder deep,
Begin to roll, and almost drown
The sweet notes, whose lulling spell
Gods and the race of mortals love so well,
  When through thy caves thou hearest music swell? 30

  But an awful pleasure bland
Spreading o'er the Thunderer's face,
When the sound climbs near his seat,
The Olympian Council sees;
As he lets his lax right hand,
Which the lightnings doth embrace,
Sink upon his mighty knees.
  And the Eagle, at the beck
Of the appeasing gracious harmony,
Droops all his sheeny, brown, deep-feather'd neck,   40
Nestling nearer to Jove's feet;
While o'er his sovereign eye
The curtains of the blue films slowly meet.
  And the white Olympus peaks
Rosily brighten, and the sooth'd Gods smile
At one another from their golden chairs;
And no one round the charmed circle speaks.
  Only the lov'd Hebe bears
The cup about, whose draughts beguile
Pain and care, with a dark store   50
Of fresh-pull'd violets wreath'd and nodding o'er;
  And her flush'd feet glow on the marble floor.

III

MARSYAS

As the sky-brightening South-wind clears the day,
And makes the mass'd clouds roll,
The music of the lyre blows away

The clouds that wrap the soul.

    Oh that Fate had let me see
That triumph of the sweet persuasive lyre,
That famous, final victory,
When jealous Pan with Marsyas did conspire;

    When, from far Panassus' side,
Young Apollo, all the pride   10
Of the Phrygian flutes to tame,
To the Phrygian highlands came:
Where the long green reed-beds sway
In the rippled waters grey
Of that solitary lake
Where Mæander's springs are born:
Whence the ridg'd pine-muffled roots
Of Messogis westward break.
Mounting westward, high and higher:
    There was held the famous strife;   20
There the Phrygian brought his flutes,
And Apollo brought his lyre,
And, when now the westering sun
Touch'd the hills, the strife was done,
And the attentive Muses said,
Marsyas! thou art vanquished.
    Then Apollo's minister
Hang'd upon a branching fir
Marsyas, that unhappy faun,
And began to whet his knife.   30
But the Mænads, who were there,
Left their friend, and with robes flowing
In the wind, and loose dark hair
O'er their polish'd bosoms blowing,
Each her ribbon'd tambourine
Flinging on the mountain sod,
With a lovely frighten'd mien
Came about the youthful God.
But he turn'd his beauteous face
Haughtily another way,   40
From the grassy sun-warm'd place,

Where in proud respose he lay,
With one arm over his head,
Watching how the whetting sped.

But aloof, on the lake strand,
Did the young Olympus stand,
Weeping at his master's end;
For the Faun had been his friend.
For he taught him how to sing,
And he taught him flute-playing. 50
Many a morning had they gone
To the glimmering mountain lakes,
And had torn up by the roots
The tall crested water reeds
With long plumes and soft brown seeds,
And had carv'd them into flutes,
Sitting on a tabled stone
Where the shoreward ripple breaks.

And he taught him how to please
The red-snooded Phrygian girls, 60
Whom the summer evening sees
Flashing in the dance's whirls
Underneath the starlit trees
In the mountain villages.
Therefore now Olympus stands,
At his master's piteous cries,
Pressing fast with both his hands
His white garment to his eyes,
Not to see Apollo's scorn.
Ah, poor Faun, poor Faun ah, poor Faun! 70

IV

APOLLO

Through the black, rushing smoke-bursts,
Quick breaks the red flame;
All Etna heaves fiercely
Her forest-cloth'd frame;

Not here, O Apollo!
Are haunts meet for thee.
But, where Helicon breaks down
In cliff to the sea,

Where the moon-silver'd inlets
Send far their light voice   10
Up the still vale of Thisbe,
O speed and rejoice!

On the sward, at the cliff-top,
Lie strewn the white flocks;
On the cliff-side the pigeons
Roost deep in the rocks.

In the moonlight the shepherds,
Soft-lull'd by the rills,
Lie wrapt in their blankets,
Asleep on the hills.   20

– What Forms are these coming
So white through the gloom?
What garments out-glistening
The gold-flower'd broom?

What sweet-breathing Presence
Out-perfumes the thyme?
What voices enrapture
The night's balmy prime? –

'Tis Apollo comes leading
His choir, The Nine.   30
– The Leader is fairest,
But all are divine.

They are lost in the hollows.
They stream up again.
What seeks on this mountain
The glorified train? –

They bathe on this mountain,
In the spring by their road.
Then on to Olympus,
Their endless abode. 40

– *Whose praise do they mention?*
Of what is it told? –
What will be for ever.
What was from of old.

First hymn they the Father
Of all things: and then
The rest of Immortals,
The action of men.

The Day in its hotness,
The strife with the palm; 50
The Night in its silence,
The Stars in their calm.

The Philosopher and the Stars

And you, ye Stars!
Who slowly begin to marshal,
As of old, in the fields of heaven,
Your distant, melancholy lines –
Have you, too, surviv'd yourselves?
Are you, too, what I fear to become?
You too once liv'd –
Your too mov'd joyfully
Among august companions
In an older world, peopled by Gods, 10
In a mightier order,
The radiant, rejoicing, intelligent Sons of Heaven!
But now, you kindle
Your lonely, cold-shining lights,

Unwilling lingerers
In the heavenly wilderness,
For a younger, ignoble world.
And renew, by necessity,
Night after night your courses,
In echoing unnear'd silence,   20
Above a race you know not.
Uncared and undelighted,
Without friend and without home.
Weary like us, though not
    Weary with our weariness.

from **Merope. A Tragedy** (1858)

The Chorus

O Son and Mother,   *str.* 1
Whom the Gods o'ershadow,
In dangerous trial,
With certainty of favour!
As erst they shadow'd
Your race's founders
From irretrievable woe:
When the seed of Lycaon
Lay forlorn, lay outcast,
Callisto and her Boy.   10

What deep-grass'd meadow   *ant.* 1
At the meeting valleys –
Where clear-flowing Ladon,
Most beautiful of waters,
Receives the river
Whose trout are vocal,
The Aroanian stream –
Without home, without mother,
Hid the babe, hid Arcas,
The nursling of the dells?   20

But the sweet-smelling myrtle,   *str.* 2
And the pink-flower'd oleander,
And the green agnus-castus,
To the West-Wind's murmur,
Rustled round his cradle;
And Maia rear'd him.
Then, a boy, he startled
In the snow-fill'd hollows
Of high Cyllene
The white mountain-birds;   30

Or surpris'd, in the glens,
The basking tortoises,
Whose strip'd shell founded
In the hands of Hermes
The glory of the lyre.

But his mother, Callisto,   *ant. 2*
In her hiding-place of the thickets
Of the lentisk and ilex,
In her rough form, fearing
The hunter on the outlook,   40
Poor changeling! trembled.
Or the children, plucking
In the thorn-chok'd gullies
Wild gooseberries, scar'd her,
The shy mountain-bear.
Or the shepherds, on slopes
With pale-spik'd lavender
And crisp thyme tufted,
Came upon her, stealing
At day-break through the dew.   50

Once, 'mid the gorges,   *str. 3*
Spray-drizzled, lonely,
Unclimb'd by man –
O'er whose cliffs the townsmen
Of crag-perch'd Nonacris
Behold in summer
The slender torrent
Of Styx come dancing,
A wind-blown thread –
By the precipices of Khelmos,   60
The fleet, desperate hunter,
The youthful Arcas, born of Zeus,
His fleeing mother,
Transform'd Callisto,
Unwitting follow'd –
And rais'd his spear.

Turning, with piteous   *ant. 3*

Distressful longing,
Sad, eager eyes,
Mutely she regarded 70
Her well-known enemy.
Low moans half utter'd
What speech refus'd her;
Tears cours'd, tears human,
Down those disfigur'd
Once human cheeks.
With unutterable foreboding
Her son, heart-stricken, ey'd her.
The Gods had pity, made them Stars.
Stars now they sparkle 80
In the northern Heaven;
The guard Arcturus,
The guard-watch'd Bear.

from **New Poems** (1867)

Dover Beach

The sea is calm to-night,
The tide is full, the moon lies fair
Upon the Straits; – on the French coast, the light
Gleams, and is gone; the cliffs of England stand,
Glimmering and vast, out in the tranquil bay.
Come to the window, sweet is the night air!
Only, from the long line of spray
Where the ebb meets the moon-blanch'd sand,
Listen! you hear the grating roar
Of pebbles which the waves suck back, and fling,   10
At their return, up the high strand,
Begin, and cease, and then again begin,
With tremulous cadence slow, and bring
The eternal note of sadness in.

   Sophocles long ago
Heard it on the Ægæan, and it brought
Into his mind the turbid ebb and flow
Of human misery; we
Find also in the sound a thought,
Hearing it by this distant northern sea.   20

The sea of faith
Was once, too, at the full, and round earth's shore
Lay like the folds of a bright girdle furl'd;
But now I only hear
Its melancholy, long, withdrawing roar,
Retreating to the breath
Of the night-wind down the vast edges drear
And naked shingles of the world.

Ah, love, let us be true

To one another! for the world, which seems   30
To lie before us like a land of dreams,
So various, so beautiful, so new,
Hath really neither joy, nor love, nor light,
Nor certitude, nor peace, nor help for pain;
And we are here as on a darkling plain
Swept with confused alarms of struggle and flight,
Where ignorant armies clash by night.

Stanzas
From the Grande Chartreuse

Through Alpine meadows soft suffused
With rain, where thick the crocus blows,
Past the dark forges long disused,
The mule-track from Saint Laurent goes.
The bridge is cross'd, and slow we ride,
Through forest, up the mountain-side.

The autumnal evening darkens round,
The wind is up, and drives the rain;
While hark! far down, with strangled sound
Doth the Dead Guiers' stream complain,   10
Where that wet smoke among the woods
Over his boiling cauldron broods.

Swift rush the spectral vapours white
Past limestone scars with ragged pines,
Shewing – then blotting from our sight.
Halt! through the cloud-drift something shines!
High in the valley, wet and drear,
The huts of Courrerie appear.

Strike leftward! cries our guide; and higher
Mounts up the stony forest-way.   20

At last the encircling trees retire;
Look! through the showery twilight grey
What pointed roofs are these advance?
A palace of the Kings of France?

Approach, for what we seek is here.
Alight and sparely sup and wait
For rest in this outbuilding near;
Then cross the sward and reach that gate;
Knock; pass the wicket! Thou art come
To the Carthusians' world-famed home.   30

The silent courts, where night and day
Into their stone-carved basins cold
The splashing icy fountains play,
The humid corridors behold,
Where ghostlike in the deepening night
Cowl'd forms brush by in gleaming white.

The chapel, where no organ's peal
Invests the stern and naked prayer.
With penitential cries they kneel
And wrestle; rising then, with bare   40
And white uplifted faces stand,
Passing the Host from hand to hand;

Each takes; and then his visage wan
Is buried in his cowl once more.
The cells – the suffering Son of Man
Upon the wall! the knee-worn floor!
And, where they sleep, that wooden bed,
Which shall their coffin be, when dead.

The library, where tract and tome
Not to feed priestly pride are there,   50
To hymn the conquering march of Rome.
Nor yet to amuse, as ours are;
They paint of souls the inner strife,
Their drops of blood, their death in life.

The garden, overgrown – yet mild
Those fragrant herbs are flowering there!
Strong children of the Alpine wild
Whose culture is the brethren's care;
Of human tasks their only one,
And cheerful works beneath the sun.   60

Those halls too, destined to contain
Each its own pilgrim host of old,
From England, Germany or Spain –
All are before me! I behold
The House, the Brotherhood austere!
And what am I, that I am here?

For rigorous teachers seized my youth,
And purged its faith, and trimm'd its fire.
Shew'd me the high white star of Truth,
There bade me gaze, and there aspire;   70
Even now their whispers pierce the gloom:
What dost thou in this living tomb?

Forgive me, masters of the mind!
At whose behest I long ago
So much unlearnt, so much resign'd!
I come not here to be your foe.
I seek these anchorites, not in ruth,
To curse and to deny your truth;

Not as their friend or child I speak!
But as on some far northern strand,   80
Thinking of his own Gods, a Greek
In pity and mournful awe might stand
Before some fallen Runic stone –
For both were faiths, and both are gone.

Wandering between two worlds, one dead,
The other powerless to be born,
With nowhere yet to rest my head,
Like these, on earth I wait forlorn.
Their faith, my tears, the world deride;
I come to shed them at their side.   90

Oh, hide me in your gloom profound
Ye solemn seats of holy pain!
Take me, cowl'd forms, and fence me round,
Till I possess my soul again!
Till free my thoughts before me roll,
Not chafed by hourly false control.

For the world cries your faith is now
But a dead time's exploded dream;
My melancholy, sciolists say,
Is a pass'd mode, an outworn theme –   100
As if the world had ever had
A faith, or sciolists been sad.

Ah, if it *be* pass'd, take away,
At least, the restlessness – the pain!
Be man henceforth no more a prey
To these out-dated stings again!
The nobleness of grief is gone –
Ah, leave us not the fret alone!

But, if you cannot give us ease,
Last of the race of them who grieve   110
Here leave us to die out with these
Last of the people who believe!
Silent, while years engrave the brow;
Silent – the best are silent now.

Achilles ponders in his tent,
The kings of modern thought are dumb;
Silent they are, though not content,
And wait to see the future come.
They have the grief men had of yore,
But they contend and cry no more.   120

Our fathers water'd with their tears
This sea of time whereon we sail;
Their voices were in all men's ears
Who pass'd within their puissant hail.

Still the same Ocean round us raves,
But we stand mute and watch the waves.

For what avail'd it, all the noise
And outcry of the former men?
Say, have their sons obtain'd more joys?
Say, is life lighter now than then?   130
The sufferers died, they left their pain;
The pangs which tortured them remain.

What helps it now, that Byron bore,
With haughty scorn which mock'd the smart,
Through Europe to the Ætolian shore
The pageant of his bleeding heart?
That thousands counted every groan,
And Europe made his woe her own?

What boots it, Shelley! that the breeze
Carried thy lovely wail away,   140
Musical through Italian trees
That fringe thy soft blue Spezzian bay?
Inheritors of thy distress
Have restless hearts one throb the less?

Or are we easier, to have read,
O Obermann! the sad, stern page,
Which tells us how thou hidd'st thy head
From the fierce tempest of thine age
In the lone brakes of Fontainebleau,
Or chalets near the Alpine snow?   150

Ye slumber in your silent grave!
The world, which for an idle day
Grace to your mood of sadness gave,
Long since hath flung her weeds away.
The eternal trifler breaks your spell;
But we – we learnt your lore too well!

There may, perhaps, yet dawn an age,
More fortunate, alas! than we,

Which without hardness will be sage,
And gay without frivolity.   160
Sons of the world, oh, haste those years;
But, till they rise, allow our tears!

Allow them! We admire with awe
The exulting thunder of your race;
You give the universe your law,
You triumph over time and space.
Your pride of life, your tireless powers,
We mark them, but they are not ours.

We are like children rear'd in shade
Beneath some old-world abbey wall   170
Forgotten in a forest-glade
And secret from the eyes of all;
Deep, deep the greenwood round them waves,
Their abbey, and its close of graves.

But where the road runs near the stream
Oft through the trees they catch a glance
Of passing troops in the sun's beam –
Pennon, and plume, and flashing lance!
Forth to the world those soldiers fare,
To life, to cities, and to war.   180

And through the woods, another way,
Faint bugle-notes from far are borne,
Where hunters gather, staghounds bay,
Round some old forest-lodge at morn;
Gay dames are there in sylvan green,
Laughter and cries – those notes between!

The banners flashing through the trees
Make their blood dance and chain their eyes;
That bugle-music on the breeze
Arrests them with a charm'd suprise.   190
Banner by turns and bugle woo:
Ye shy recluses, follow too!

O children, what do ye reply? –
'Action and pleasure, will ye roam
Through these secluded dells to cry
And call us? but too late ye come!
Too late for us your call ye blow
Whose bent was taken long ago.

'Long since we pace this shadow'd nave;
We watch those yellow tapers shine,   200
Emblems of hope over the grave,
In the high altar's depth divine;
The organ carries to our ear
Its accents of another sphere.

'Fenced early in this cloistral round
Of reverie, of shade, of prayer,
How should we grow in other ground?
How should we flower in foreign air?
Pass, banners, pass, and bugles, cease!
And leave our desert to its peace!'   210

from **Poems** (1877)

Switzerland

1 MEETING

Again I see my bliss at hand,
The town, the lake are here;
My Marguerite smiles upon the strand
Unalter'd with the year.

I know that graceful figure fair,
That cheek of languid hue;
I know that soft, enkerchief'd hair,
And those sweet eyes of blue.

Again I spring to make my choice;
Again in tones of ire
I hear a God's tremendous voice: 10
'Be counsell'd, and retire.'

Ye guiding Powers who join and part,
What would ye have with me?
Ah, warn some more ambitious heart,
And let the peaceful be!

2 PARTING

Ye storm-winds of autumn!
Who rush by, who shake
The window, and ruffle
The gleam-lighted lake;
Who cross to the hill-side
Thin-sprinkled with farms,
Where the high woods strip sadly
Their yellowing arms –
Ye are bound for the mountains!

Ah! with you let me go   10
Where your cold, distant barrier,
The vast range of snow,
Through the loose clouds lifts dimly
Its white peaks in air –
How deep is their stillness!
Ah, would I were there!

But on the stairs what voice is this I hear,
Buoyant as morning, and as morning clear?
Say, has some wet bird-haunted English lawn
Lent it the music of its trees at dawn?   20
Or was it from some sun-fleck'd mountain-brook
That the sweet voice its upland clearness took?
          Ah! it comes nearer –
          Sweet notes, this way!

Hark! fast by the window
The rushing winds go,
To the ice-cumber'd gorges,
The vast seas of snow.
There the torrents drive upward
Their rock-strangled hum;   30
There the avalanche thunders
The hoarse torrent dumb.
– I come, O ye mountains!
Ye torrents, I come!

But who is this, by the half-open'd door,
Whose figure casts a shadow on the floor?
The sweet blue eyes – the soft, ash-colour'd hair –
The cheeks that still their gentle paleness wear –
The lovely lips, with their arch smile that tells
The unconquer'd joy in which her spirit dwells –   40
          Ah! they bend nearer –
          Sweet lips, this way!

Hark! the wind rushes past us.
Ah! with that let me go
To the clear, waning hill-side,

Unspotted by snow,
There to watch, o'er the sunk vale,
The frore mountain-wall,
Where the niched snow-bed sprays down
Its powdery fall.   50
There its dusky blue clusters
The aconite spreads;
There the pines slope, the cloud-strips
Hung soft in their heads.
No life but, at moments,
The mountain-bee's hum.
– I come, O ye mountains!
Ye pine-woods, I come!

Forgive me! forgive me!
   Ah, Marguerite, fain   60
Would these arms reach to clasp thee!
   But see! 'tis in vain.

In the void air, towards thee,
   My stretch'd arms are cast;
But a sea rolls between us –
   Our different past!

To the lips, ah! of others,
   Those lips have been prest,
And others, ere I was,
   Were strain'd to that breast;   70

Far, far from each other
   Our spirits have grown.
And what heart knows another?
   Ah! who knows his own?

Blow, ye winds! lift me with you!
   I come to the wild.
Fold closely, O Nature!
   Thine arms round thy child.

To thee only God granted

A heart ever new –   80
To all always open,
  To all always true.

Ah, calm me! restore me!
  And dry up my tears
On thy high mountain-platforms,
  Where morn first appears,

Where the white mists, for ever,
  Are spread and upfurl'd;
In the stir of the forces
  Whence issued the world.   90

3 A FAREWELL

My horse's feet beside the lake,
Where sweet the unbroken moonbeams lay,
Sent echoes through the night to wake
Each glistening strand, each heath-fringed bay.

The poplar avenue was pass'd,
And the roof'd bridge that spans the stream.
Up the steep street I hurried fast,
Led by thy taper's starlike beam.

I came! I saw thee rise! – the blood
Pour'd flushing to thy languid cheek.   10
Lock'd in each other's arms we stood,
In tears, with hearts too full to speak.

Days flew; – ah, soon I could discern
A trouble in thine alter'd air!
Thy hand lay languidly in mine,
Thy cheek was grave, thy speech grew rare.

I blame thee not! – this heart, I know,
To be long loved was never framed;
For something in its depth doth glow
Too strange, too restless, too untamed.   20

And women – things that live and move
Mined by the fever of the soul –
They seek to find in those they love
Stern strength, and promise of control.

They ask not kindness, gentle ways;
These they themselves have tried and known.
They ask a soul which never sways
With the blind gusts that shake their own.

I too have felt the load I bore
In a too strong emotion's sway;   30
I too have wish'd, no woman more,
This starting, feverish heart away.

I too have long'd for trenchant force
And will like a dividing spear;
Have praised the keen, unscrupulous course,
Which knows no doubt, which feels no fear.

But in the world I learnt, what there
Thou too wilt surely one day prove,
That will, that energy, though rare,
Are yet far, far less rare than love.   40

Go, then! – till time and fate impress
This truth on thee, be mine no more!
They will! – for thou, I feel, not less
Than I, wast destined to this lore.

We school our manners, act our parts –
But He, who sees us through and through,
Knows that the bent of both our hearts
Was to be gentle, tranquil true.

And though we wear out life, alas!
Distracted as a homeless wind,   50
In beating where we must not pass,
In seeking what we shall not find;

Yet we shall one day gain, life past,
Clear prospect o'er our being's whole;
Shall see ourselves, and learn at last
Our true affinities of soul.

We shall not then deny a course
To every thought the mass ignore;
We shall not then call hardness force,
Nor lightness wisdom any more.   60

Then, in the eternal Father's smile,
Our soothed, encouraged souls will dare
To seem as free from pride and guile,
As good, as generous, as they are.

Then we shall know our friends; – though much
Will have been lost – the help in strife,
The thousand sweet, still joys of such
As hand in hand face earthly life –

Though these be lost, there will be yet
A sympathy august and pure;   70
Ennobled by a vast regret,
And by contrition seal'd thrice sure.

And we, whose ways were unlike here,
May then more neighbouring courses ply;
May to each other be brought near
And greet across infinity.

How sweet, unreach'd by earthly jars,
My sister! to maintain with thee
The hush among the shining stars,
The calm upon the moonlit sea!   80

How sweet to feel, on the boon air,
All our unquiet pulses cease!
To feel that nothing can impair
The gentleness, the thirst for peace –

The gentleness too rudely hurl'd
On this wild earth of hate and fear;
The thirst for peace a raving world
Would never let us satiate here.

4 ISOLATION. TO MARGUERITE

We were apart; yet, day by day,
I bade my heart more constant be.
I bade it keep the world away,
And grow a home for only thee;
Nor fear'd but thy love likewise grew,
Like mine, each day more tried, more true.

The fault was grave! I might have known,
What far too soon, alas! I learn'd –
The heart can bind itself alone,
And faith may well be unreturn'd.   10
Self-sway'd our feelings ebb and swell –
Thou lov'st no more; – Farewell! Farewell!

Farewell! – and thou, thou lonely heart,
Which never yet without remorse
Even for a moment didst depart
From thy remote and spheréd course
To haunt the place where passions reign –
Back to thy solitude again!

Back! with the conscious thrill of shame
Which Luna felt, that summer-night,   20
Flash through her pure immortal frame,
When she forsook the starry height
To hang over Endymion's sleep
Upon the pine-grown Latmian steep.

Yet she, chaste queen, had never proved
How vain a thing is mortal love,
Wandering in Heaven, far removed;
But thou has long had place to prove
This truth – to prove, and make thine own:
'Thou hast been, shalt be, art, alone.'   30

Or, if not quite alone, yet they
Which touch thee are unmating things –
Ocean and clouds and night and day;
Lorn autumns and triumphant springs;
And life, and others' joy and pain,
And love, if love, of happier men.

Of happier men – for they, at least,
Have *dream'd* two human hearts might blend
In one, and were through faith released
From isolation without end   40
Prolong'd; nor knew, although not less
Alone than thou, their loneliness.

5 TO MARGUERITE. CONTINUED

Yes! in the sea of life enisled,
With echoing straits between us thrown,
Dotting the shoreless watery wild,
We mortal millions live *alone*.
The islands feel the enclasping flow,
And then their endless bounds they know.

But when the moon their hollows lights,
And they are swept by balms of spring,
And in their glens, on starry nights,
The nightingales divinely sing;   10
And lovely notes, from shore to shore,
Across the sounds and channels pour –

Oh! then a longing like despair
Is to their farthest caverns sent;
For surely once, they feel, we were
Parts of a single continent!
Now round us spreads the watery plain –
Oh might our marges meet again!

Who order'd, that their longing's fire
Should be, as soon as kindled, cool'd?   20
Who renders vain their deep desire? –
A God, a God their severance ruled!

And bade betwixt their shores to be
The unplumb'd, salt estranging sea.

6 ABSENCE

In this fair stranger's eyes of grey
Thine eyes, my love! I see.
I shiver; for the passing day
Had borne me far from thee.

This is the curse of life! that not
A nobler, calmer train
Of wiser thought and feelings blot
Our passions from our brain;

But each day brings its petty dust
Our soon-choked souls to fill;   10
And we forget because we must,
And not because we will.

I struggle towards the light; and ye,
Once-long'd-for storms of love!
If with the light ye cannot be,
I bear that ye remove.

I struggle towards the light – but oh,
While yet the night is chill,
Upon time's barren, stormy flow.
Stay with me, Marguerite, still!   20

7 THE TERRACE AT BERNE

(composed ten years after the preceding)

Ten years! – and to my waking eye
Once more the roofs of Berne appear;
The rocky banks, the terrace high,
The stream! – and do I linger here?

The clouds are on the Oberland,
The Jungfrau snows look faint and far;

But bright are those green fields at hand,
And through those fields comes down the Aar,

And from the blue twin-lakes it comes,
Flows by the town, the church-yard fair;   10
And 'neath the garden-walk it hums,
The house! – and is my Marguerite there?

Ah, shall I see thee, while a flush
Of startled pleasure floods thy brow,
Quick through the oleanders brush,
And clap thy hands, and cry: *'Tis thou!*

Or hast thou long since wander'd back,
Daughter of France! to France, thy home;
And flitted down the flowery track
Where feet like thine too lightly come?   20

Doth riotous laughter now replace
Thy smile, and rouge, with stony glare,
Thy cheek's soft hue, and fluttering lace
The kerchief that enwound thy hair?

Or is it over? – art though dead? –
Dead! – and no warning shiver ran
Across my heart, to say thy thread
Of life was cut, and closed thy span!

Could from earth's ways that figure slight
Be lost, and I not feel 'twas so?   30
Of that fresh voice the gay delight
Fail from earth's air, and I not know?

Or shall I find thee still, but changed,
But not the Marguerite of thy prime?
With all thy being re-arranged,
Pass'd through the crucible of time:

With spirit vanish'd, beauty waned,
And hardly yet a glance, a tone,

A gesture – anything – retain'd
Of all that was my Marguerite's own?   40

I will not know! For wherefore try
To things by mortal course that live
A shadowy durability,
For which they were not meant, to give?

Like driftwood spars, which meet and pass
Upon the boundless ocean-plain,
So the sea of life, alas!
Man meets man – meets, and quits again.

I knew it when my life was young;
I feel it still now youth is o'er. –   50
The mists are on the mountain hung,
And Marguerite I shall see no more.

Notes

p. 3 **The Strayed Reveller** Probably written in 1847. The setting is that of Homer's *Odyssey* Book 10; Ulysses is living with the enchantress Circe who serves visitors a wine that transforms them into animals. In the Romantic period writers began to use Circe's wine as a symbol of inspiration. **38 Iacchus:** Greek god identified with Dionysus or Bacchus. **135 Tiresias**: a Theban, struck blind by the goddess Hera but compensated with the gift of prophecy. **142 The doom of Thebes**: which Tiresias foresees is the topic of three tragedies by Sophocles. **143 Centaurs**: legendary creatures, with the lower body of a horse and upper body of a man, who lived on Mount Pelion in Thessaly. **183 Chorasmian stream**: River Oxus in Central Asia. **228 Lapithae**: the Centaurs attended a wedding given by the Lapithae and a battle resulted. **231 Alcmena's dreadful son**: Hercules who fought the Centaurs during his labours. **259 Argo**: Argonauts' ship in quest for the golden fleece. **261 Silenus**: a satyr, a creature part beast part man.

p. 12 **Mycerinus** Probably written in 1847. Until 1.78 the poem is a dramatic monologue spoken by the 4th Dynasty Egyptian King Men-kau-Ra (called Mycerinus by Herodotus) who ruled *c.*2500 BC. The monologue uses the stanza of Wordsworth's 'Laodamia', whose serene acceptance of divine justice Arnold's poem questions.

p. 15 **The Forsaken Merman**: Probably written in 1847, when Hans Christian Andersen visited England and Mary Howitt published her translation of Andersen's autobiography; this describes Andersen's poem based on the Danish ballad 'Agnes and the Merman'.

p. 19 **To a Friend** Written in 1848; the friend is almost certainly Clough. **2 old man**: Homer. **3 Wide Prospect ... Asian Fen**: Arnold thought the Greek word 'Europe' meant 'wide prospect' and 'Asia' derived from the Greek word for mud. **4 Tmolus**: Smyrna, under Mount Tmolus, was Homer's birthplace. **6 slave**: the Stoic philosopher Epictetus (AD 60–140). Born a slave, and lame, he taught in Rome until the Emperor Domitian banished philosophers from Italy.

He then taught at Nicopolis (in Greece) where Arrian recorded his lectures. **9 even-balanced soul**: Sophocles, born at Colonus in 496 BC.

p. 20 **Resignation. To Fausta** Probably written in 1848, though it may recall a Lake District walk with Jane Arnold in 1843 when Jane's engagement had been broken off. In 1848 another sister, Mary, was widowed. Another of the *Strayed Reveller* poems, 'A Question. To Fausta', is addressed to this figure who feels a similar dissatisfaction with life. The Stoic argument reflects Arnold's reading of Epictetus and the *Bhagavad-Gita*. **7 Lydian**: country in Asia Minor through which Crusaders travelled to Jerusalem. **13 Euxine**: the Black Sea.

p. 28 **Too Late** Later reprinted as the second poem in the 'Faded Leaves' sequence of love poems.

p. 29 **Stanzas in Memory of the Author of 'Obermann'** Written September to November 1849. Étienne Pivert de Senancour (1770–1846) published his novel *Oberman* (retitled *Obermann* in 1833) in 1804. The hero is an introspective recluse who, like Senancour in the 1790s, takes refuge from the modern world in rural Switzerland. *Oberman* was rediscovered by Sainte-Beuve and George Sand in the 1830s. In 1867 Arnold would publish 'Obermann Once More', a more optimistic sequel. **5 baths**: Arnold describes a walk from Thun, through the Gemmi Pass and the spa at Leukerbad (or 'Baths of Leuk'), to Leuk in the Rhone valley. **89 son of Thetis**: Achilles. **114 Jaman**: Mount Jaman overlooks Vevey, on Lake Leman; Obermann settles in a chalet at 'Immenström near Vevey' in Letter 66 of the novel. **164 Meillerie** village by Lake Leman. **179 Capital of Pleasure**: Paris.

p. 36 **Sohrab and Rustum. An Episode** Conceived in 1851 but probably written in January to April 1853. Arnold found the story in an essay on Firdousi by Sainte-Beuve. Firdousi (*c.* 935–1020 AD) wrote the Persian epic the *Shahnama* (Book of Kings) and was seen as 'The Homer of the East'; Arnold's poem resembles a fragment of Homeric epic. **3 Tartar**: Tartar, Turk, and Scythian are alternative modern terms for the people of ancient Túrán in Central Asia; Sohrab accompanies their army in an attack on the Persian forces of Kai-Khosroo (in Greek: Cyrus). In Arnold's sources this episode occurs in the reign of Kai-Khosroo's predecessor, Kai-Kaoos (Greek: Cyaxares), King of Persia *c.*634–594 BC. **38 Afrasiab**: King of Túrán. Túrán and Irán (Persia) were the two great countries of north-west Asia, to the north and south of the River Oxus. **42 Ader-baijan**: Arnold locates Firdousi's 'Samengán' in Kurdish Azerbaijan, on the western boundary of Iran. **50 Rustum**: principal hero of the *Shahnama*, 'the Persian Hercules', who lived in Seistan on the eastern border of Iran. **679 Zal**: born with ominously white hair, Zál was left to die but was rescued and brought up by a Símurgh or Griffin. **880 Orgunjè**: modern Khiva.

p. 58 *Cadmus and Harmonia* Originally printed in 1852 as the 2nd song of Callicles in 'Empedocles on Etna' (1.2.427–60), where it immediately followed 'The Chant of Empedocles'; probably written 1851–2. Printed separately in Arnold's editions of 1853, 1854 and 1857, and in his *Selected Poems* from 1878. **10 Cadmus**: founder of the Greek city of Thebes. He married Harmonia and had four daughters: Semele, Ino, Autonoe, and Agave. **12 all their ills**: Semele was consumed by Zeus's lighting. Ino was driven mad and drowned herself. Autonoe's son Actaeon was transformed into a stag and killed by his own hounds. Agave's son Pentheus was torn to pieces by worshippers of Dionysus who included Agave. **14 Spinx**: in the reign of Laius, great-grandson of Cadmus, Thebes was plagued by the monstrous Sphinx. Oedipus, the lost son of Laius, defeated the Sphinx but unwittingly killed his father and married his mother. **16 Ismenus**: river which flows through Thebes. **25 Muses sang**: Pindar's 3rd Pythian Ode states that the unhappy life of Cadmus was redeemed by the 'supreme happiness' of hearing the Muses. **31 chang'd forms**: in Ovid's *Metamorphoses* Cadmus reaches Illyria where he prays to appease divine anger at his killing of the serpent of Mars by himself becoming a snake.

p. 59 *The Scholar Gipsy* Probably written in the autumn of 1852 or summer of 1853, though Arnold had known the story since the mid-1840s. Arnold wrote to his brother Tom in 1857 that the poem was 'meant to fix the remembrance of those delightful wanderings of ours in the Cumner Hills' as Oxford undergraduates in 1843. **31 Glanvil's book**: Joseph Glanvill, *The Vanity of Dogmatizing* (1661), in which this story is used to warn against overly dogmatic scientific assertion. **69 Cumner hills**: open country in Berkshire, immediately to the west of Oxford. **129 Christ-Church**: an Oxford college. **149 Genius**: the spirit or daemon which presides over each human life. **182 One**: Goethe, according to Arnold in 1883; a case has also been made for

Tennyson and Leopardi. **208 Dido**: in Book 6 of Virgil's *Aeneid*, Aeneas attempts to approach his former lover Dido in the underworld; she rejects him. **232 Tyrian**: from Tyre (in modern Lebanon), port of the Phoenicians who flourished in the eastern Mediterranean from *c.*1200 BC until their conquest by Alexander the Great. **238 Chian**: from Chios, Greek island famous for wine and figs. **244 Midland**: Mediterranean. **245 Syrtes**: sandbanks off coast of North Africa. **249 Iberians**: people of southern Spain.

p. 67 *The Harp Player on Etna* Collective title for the songs of Callicles from 'Empedocles on Etna' (except 'Cadmus and Harmonia') when Arnold put them back into print in 1855. Probably written 1851–2. Callicles is a strayed reveller who has left a party to follow Empedocles as he climbs Mount Etna; his songs try to alleviate the philosopher's depression.

p. 67 **I The Last Glen**: Originally the 1st song in 'Empedocles on Etna' (1.2.36–76), immediately preceding 'The Chant of Empedocles'; Arnold echoes Pindar's 3rd Nemean Ode on the education of Achilles. **23 Pelion**: mountain in Thessaly; home of the Centaurs, legendary creatures half man, half horse. **24 Chiron**: wise Centaur who educated several Greek heroes, including Achilles, the chief Greek warrior in the Trojan War. **33 Phthia**: town in Thessaly where Achilles was born. **70 Peleus**: father of Achilles. **39 Elysian**: Elysium was the posthumous heaven of the Greeks.

p. 68 **II Typho**: originally the 3rd song (2.37–88), sung as Empedocles reaches the crater. Based on Pindar's 1st Pythian Ode ('The Power of Music') but using the strophe/antistrophe pattern of a Greek tragic chorus. **5 Typho**: giant who made war on the gods; Jove imprisoned him under Mount Etna. **17 Cilician**: Cilicia was a country in Asia Minor where Typho previously lived. **18 Mount of Gore**: Mount Haemus which separates Thessaly from Thrace; Typho's blood (Greek *haima*) fell on it. **21 Sicilian**: Mount Etna is on the coast of Sicily. **32 Thunderer**: Jove. **34 Olympian**: Greeks gods lived on Mount Olympus. **38 Eagle**: the eagle, king of birds, was a symbol of the power of Jove, king of gods. **48 Hebe**: daughter of Jove and Juno; handmaiden of the gods for whom she pours out nectar.

p. 69 **III Marsyas**: Originally the 4th song (2.121–90), sung as

Empedocles takes off the symbols of his status as a poet. Arnold follows the story as given in the *Fabulae* of Hyginus: the satyr (or 'Faun') Marsyas, famous for his skill on the flute, or pipe, is defeated by Apollo's performance on the lyre. **8 Pan**: Greek god of shepherds who invented the Pan pipe. **9 Parnassus**: mountain in Greece associated with Apollo and the Muses. **11 Phrygian**: Marsyas lived in Phrygia, a country in Asia Minor; the 'Phrygian mode' of music was stirring and emotional, unlike the 'Dorian mode' of mainland Greece. **16 Maeander**: a river which flows from Phrygia, past mount Messogis, into the Aegean. **27 Apollo's minister**: Hyginus says that 'a Scythian' carried out the flaying, or stripping off of skin. **31 Maenads**: female followers of Dionysus.

p. 71 **IV Apollo**: Originally the 5th song (2.417–68) which ends the play; reprinted in *Selected Poems* from 1878 as 'Apollo Musagetes' (Apollo the Leader of the Muses). **7 Helicon**: mountain in Boeotia; site of the sanctuary of the nine Muses, goddesses of poetry, philosophy and art. **11 Thisbe**: town in Boeotia.

p. 73 ***The Philosopher and the Stars*** The only words spoken by Empedocles which Arnold kept in print between 1853 and 1867. Probably written in the summer of 1849; printed as 'Empedocles on Etna' 2.276–300 in 1852 and separately in 1855 (where it immediately followed 'Despondency').

p. 73 ***Chorus*** ('O Son and Mother') Spoken by Messenian maidens in Arnold's verse tragedy *Merope* (lines 1596–678), published December 1857. Polyphontes became King of Messenia by killing his brother Cresphontes. Cresphontes's widow, Merope, saved their son, Aepytus, by sending him to Arcadia. Aepytus grows up and returns to Messenia, claiming to have murdered the legitimate heir. Believing this, Merope almost kills him. But she discovers his real identity and Aepytus goes on to kill Polyphontes. This chorus is spoken shortly after her discovery. **8 Lycaon**: King of Arcadia and ancestor of Merope. **10 Callisto**: the daughter of Lycaon who was loved by Zeus and gave birth to Arcas. Zeus's jealous wife Hera transformed Callisto into a bear, and Arcas was brought up by Maia, an earth goddess. Out hunting he met his mother, as a bear, and nearly killed her. **13 Ladon**: river in Arcadia. **17 Aroanian stream**: tributary of the Ladon that contains fish which, according to Pausanias, make a noise like a thrush. **29 Cyllenê**:

mountain in Arcadia, where Hermes was born. **39 lentisk**: aromatic tree. **56 Nonacris**: town in Arcadia, near the River Styx. **61 Khelmos**: modern Greek name for the Aroanian Hills.

p. 78 ***Dover Beach*** Published in 1867; written either in 1851 when Arnold twice briefly visited Dover during his honeymoons (for which there is some circumstantial manuscript evidence) or, alternatively, between 1857 and 1867 (which would explain why the poem was not published in any of the five editions of Arnold's poetry between 1852 and 1857); Arnold spent a summer holiday with his wife at Dover in 1857, writing *Merope* and studying Sophocles. **15 Sophocles**: Athenian dramatist (496–06 BC); see the 3rd chorus of *Antigone*. **37 ignorant armies**: allusion to Thucydides's account of the night battle at Epipolae during the Athenian expedition to Sicily (415–13 BC) in the Peloponnesian War.

p. 79 ***Stanzas from the Grande Chartreuse*** Published in *Fraser's Magazine* April 1855, in book form in 1867. Arnold visited the Grande Chartreuse, a Carthusian monastery in the French Alps, in September 1851. He worked on the poem in 1852, possibly using material from the late 1840s, but probably did not complete it until 1854–5. **10 Dead Guier's stream**: the stream known as the Guiers Mort rises near the monastery and falls into a 'cauldron' of rock in the valley below. **42 Passing the Host**: Arnold is wrong about several details of Carthusian practice; the monks pass not the Host but the Pax tablet. **67 rigorous teachers**: Arnold is probably thinking of his Broad Church upbringing: his father had been a leader of this liberal school of Christian thought and an opponent of the 'High Church' Oxford Movement with its sympathy for such Roman Catholic practices as monasticism; *Fraser's* was a Broad Church journal in the 1850s. Arnold may, however, also be referring to influences that unsettled his religious belief, such as Carlyle, Goethe, and Spinoza. **83 Runic stone**: stone inscribed with the Runic writing of pre-Christian Germanic tribes; since Scandanavian paganism did not die out until after the twelfth century AD, the Greek traveller is, like Arnold at the Grande Chartreuse, a relatively modern tourist. **99 sciolists**: superficial pretenders to knowledge. **115 Achilles**: Greek hero of the Trojan War who withdrew to his tent after a quarrel. **134 Byron**: English poet (1788–1824) who died at Missolonghi, in the Aetolian region of Greece. **139 Shelley**: English poet (1792–1822) who was drowned off the Italian coast near La Spezia. **146 Obermann**: see 'Stanzas in Memory of the Author of "Obermann" '.

p. 86 *Switzerland*: Arnold worked on this poem for nearly thirty years, repeatedly revising it, and publishing it in its final form only in 1877. At different time nine poems were included in the sequence, the first of which (not included in the final version) was originally published in 1849 as an independent lyric. Five more poems were printed in 1852. The lyric sequence 'Switzerland' first appeared as such in 1853, then consisting of six poems. The sequence grew to seven poems in 1854, and to eight in 1857. In 1867 Arnold published 'The Terrace at Berne', though not as part of the sequence, adding it and dropping 'A Dream' in 1869. Finally, in 1877, he dropped 'To My Friends', and settled on a seven-poem sequence. Arnold visited Thun, in Switzerland, in 1848 and 1849 and the poem may possibly be based on a real experience. Alternatively he may be providing a fictitious equivalent for a previous love affair or constructuring an entirely fictive narrative. **Isolation. To Marquerite: 20 Luna**: the moon goddess fell in love with Endymion, a shepherd on Mount Latmos.